IRAQ

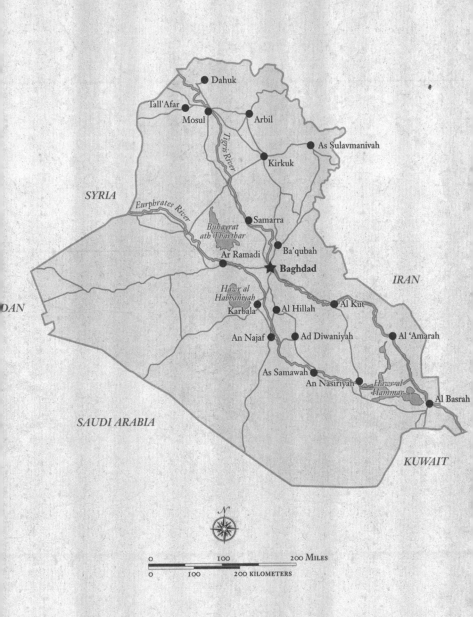

PRAISE FOR MIKE TUCKER

"RONIN *by Mike Tucker, a gripping book on Marine snipers in Iraq, is along with* Ghost Wars, *one of the top ten books since September 11th."*

"RONIN *is a must read, the unvarnished stories of Marine scout/ snipers who use their wits and highly specialized skills to track and take down insurgents in the urban jungles of Iraq."*

"Among Warriors in Iraq *is hard-boiled and absorbing. . . . Mike Tucker also has Hemingway's eye for description, particularly of warriors."*

"*In* Hell Is Over: Voices of the Kurds after Saddam, *Mike Tucker tells a story we should know, but would not except for his bravery."*

"The Long Patrol *is a refreshing, overdue look at what is sadly one of Asia's least-reported stories: the Burmese junta's continuing oppression of its ethnic minorities. Mike Tucker crafts a thoughtful, humane, no-nonsense story about the plight of the Karen freedom fighters."*

"*A classic on deep reconnaissance,* The Long Patrol *should be required reading at the John F. Kennedy Special Warfare Center & School."*

OPERATION HOTEL CALIFORNIA

THE CLANDESTINE WAR INSIDE IRAQ

MIKE TUCKER   CHARLES FADDIS

THE LYONS PRESS
Guilford, Connecticut

An imprint of The Globe Pequot Press

The Lyons Press is an imprint of The Globe Pequot Press.

Mike Tucker is the author of this book. Charles "Sam" Faddis was his main source. The views, thoughts, and opinions expressed in the introduction and epilogue are the views, thoughts, and opinions of the author.

Text designed by Sheryl P. Kober

Excerpt on page 173 is from *Straits of Malacca and other poems* Copyright © 2008 by Michael James Tucker

Map © Morris Book Publishing, LLC

Library of Congress Cataloging-in-Publication Data

Tucker, Mike, correspondent.
  Operation hotel California : the clandestine war inside Iraq / Mike Tucker, Charles Faddis.
     p. cm.
  Includes bibliographical references.
  ISBN 978-1-59921-366-8
  1. Iraq War, 2003—Campaigns. 2. United States. Central Intelligence Agency—Iraq. I. Faddis, Charles. II. Title.
  DS79.76.T82 2009
  956.7044'38—dc22

                                        2008033756

Printed in the United States of America

10 9 8 7 6 5 4 3 2

This book is dedicated in memory of
Captain James Faddis, United States Navy.

For the Kurds who fought from 1961 to 2003 for the Kurdish
Revolution, from the back alleys of Mosul to the ridgelines
and peaks of the Gara and Zagros mountains.

And for the Kurdish children who are growing up in
highlands their fathers and grandfathers liberated from
Saddam, with the aid of Sam Faddis and his
CIA counterterrorist team on Operation Hotel California,
July 2002–May 2003.

CONTENTS

AUTHOR'S NOTE ON OPERATIONAL SECURITY:

To protect their lives and families, none of the Central Intelligence Agency counterterrorists, case officers, U.S. Special Operations commandos, and U.S. Special Forces commandos behind enemy lines in Iraq from July 2002 through May 2003 are named in this book. The team leader retired from the CIA in May 2008. At his request, he is named "Sam" in this book; his real name is Charles S. Faddis.

All statements of fact, opinion, or analysis expressed are those of the author and do not reflect the official positions or views of the CIA or any other U.S. Government agency. Nothing in the contents should be construed as asserting or implying U.S. Government authentication of information or Agency endorsement of the author's views. The material in this book has been reviewed by the CIA to prevent the disclosure of classified information. Mike Tucker was not required to, and did not, submit his portion (in black text) of *Operation Hotel California* to the CIA for prepublication review.

INTRODUCTION

THE COUNTERTERRORISTS

by Mike Tucker

They were American counterterrorists on the mission of their lives, one that would test their resolve, cunning, and resourcefulness like no other clandestine operation they'd ever carried out in the Near East.

Americans paid well to take down Al-Qaeda for a living, they were damned good at tracking and killing terrorists and slipping away like ghosts, night and day. A mission was only successful if they went unseen.

The counterterrorists read Hemingway and Homer and Thucydides, smuggled guns and plastic explosives and food into Iraq past armed border guards of the American NATO ally, Turkey, and listened to "Lowrider" and "I Walk the Line" and "Gimme Shelter," the music they'd rolled with stateside on the streets and highlands and deserts of their youth, smoking their first cigarettes and drinking their first whiskey, coming of age just after the Vietnam War ripped America apart like nothing else since President Abraham Lincoln had declared that a house divided cannot stand in another generation, in another century. Yet the music of their youth from the 1960s and 1970s kept them in good stead in Iraq thirty years later, like a talisman rocking from across the far dark waters of the Mediterranean and the Atlantic, helping them stay alive in the clandestine war in Iraq. The first loves of a man's youth run through all the currents of his life.

They were American counterterrorists from the Central Intelligence Agency, and they crossed the Harburr River from Turkey into Kurdistan on a burning hot day, July 10, 2002, the beginning of the most complex and dangerous covert operation in American history.

The counterterrorists, with a wit singular to their profession, defined deconstructionism as how to deconstruct a suicide bomb and keep people from being blown to kingdom come by Al-Qaeda, which is an outstanding definition, and the only one that saves lives. They were just as home in a three-piece suit as they were in blue jeans and ragged T-shirts. Their women were understanding and patient and kind, and, as an Australian counterterrorist once told me, "Us counterterrorists are from Mars, and our Aphrodites are from Venus. Know this: When Mars and Venus come together, intergalactic magic is happening. Women may be from Venus, but they feel like heaven on earth."

Born on both coasts of the United States, the counterterrorists also hailed from the heartland and mountains of America. Depending on the country and the climate, they wore turbans or baseball caps; Aussie outback range coats or $1,500 trench coats with tailor-made inner pouches for .45 caliber clips; Bogart the Cool Maltese Falcon–style fedoras or jazz master Charles Mingus hip cat porkpie hats; jeans or three-piece suits; combat boots or custom-made wing tips; professional divers' watches or cheap-cheap Bangkok specials that look like a Rolex and run like a fat man on Quaaludes.

Aye, they were counterterrorists and masters of disguise, known to blend in and fade out of any street corner, friends to

shadows in every world capital, and able to hot-wire a motorcycle and make swift retreat on any terrain, for as a British
counterterrorist once said, "Better to make a good run than
a bad stand. Fuck the macho bullshit—sometimes you have
to make like a ghost and disappear. The odds are not always
in your favor, living is better than dying, and you will get
another chance to take down the terrorists if you give yourself
another chance to take. As long as you remember that, you'll
go a long way. Humility is a beautiful trait, mate."

Nearly all bearded and all fluent in the language of survival, the Americans carried sidearms and assault rifles and
knives behind enemy lines in Iraq. They'd been traveling
soldiers and Special Operations commandos in past lives,
studied martial arts and hand-to-hand combat like a heart
transplant specialist studies arteries, and were skilled in all
clandestine arts.

The American counterterrorists' main mission behind
enemy lines in Iraq was, in Sam's words, "to go places where
the United States government does not want to admit it has
sent anyone, acquire intelligence, scope the situation, and
leave without anyone ever knowing we were there. When and
if we get told to go past that, our methodology is to scope the
target, get way down in the weeds, learn it inside and out, and
then strike in a way that no one can defend against and no
one ever sees coming. The best engagement is one which ends
before the enemy even knows it started. Yes, if we are jammed,
and everything has gone to shit, we are ready, able, and willing
to do whatever it takes to make sure we are the ones who live
to tell the war stories, but when we are drawing weapons and
firing, it is a very bad day."

I've known more British counterterrorists than Americans, in truth. The Brits have lived in dusty shacks and hovels in God's sandbox, the Near East, and on cobblestone lanes in Madrid named after Cervantes, and in mansions in Italy acquired from heroin dealers who'd financed the mortgages with terrorist gold. When the Englishmen took down the terrorists, aye, then they owned the mansions. Beguiling way to gain splendid views of the Mediterranean, but as a British counterterrorist said of that mission, "Life is full of surprises and some of them are pleasant." 'Tis, indeed.

The Americans were eight together on that summer day, entering Iraq covertly. Eight highly skilled counterterrorist officers of the CIA, entered Kurdistan on July 10, 2002, to strike and kill Al-Qaeda, and to take down Saddam Hussein's Baathist dictatorship.

The U.S. government told other governments that they did not exist; other governments told the U.S. government that their ghosts did not exist, either. Makes for one helluva ghost story at the end of the day: Dead terrorists see no counterterrorists, but the counterterrorists see terrorists and kill them dead. Counterterrorist officers, spooks with a bad attitude, a throwing knife, and a sidearm.

The first law of counterterrorism: You either kill the terrorists or they kill you.

The second law of counterterrorism: Dead terrorists launch no suicide bomb attacks.

The third law: Dead terrorists recruit no terrorists to launch suicide bomb attacks.

The fourth law: Dead terrorists open no offshore accounts.

The fifth law: Dead terrorists build no terrorist cells.

The sixth law: Dead terrorists hijack no planes.

And the seventh law—When in doubt, remember the first law of counterterrorism: Kill the terrorists, and then enjoy single-malt scotch and other delights.

Moses may have required the Ten Commandments, but counterterrorists, whether they are Zen Buddhists or Christians or atheists, only need seven laws. To stay alive as a counterterrorist, you have to think smarter and fight harder than any spy in any movie, beyond James Bond and Jason Bourne. (Will Hollywood ever name a spy, even one with amnesia, with initials other than J. B.? Only the Shadow knows. And the Shadow is a counterterrorist.)

In Marine infantry, we called them ghost killers. We'd see the clandestine counterterrorist officers and U.S. Special Operations commandos getting on or off choppers in Okinawa and Korea, and we never saw the choppers in daylight. That was two decades ago, when the Japanese Red Army brigade terrorists had thrown down a death threat on all Marines in Asia, so the counterterrorists came to take down the Japanese terrorists threatening to kill us, the thinking being, better for our counterterrorists to kill the terrorists before the terrorists kill any Marines, or any other Americans and our allies. We knew the Japanese Red Army brigades meant to kill us, as they had killed people at airports in Europe—and enjoyed doing it—so we had no doubt that they meant to kill us Marines in Asia.

"Don't talk to those dudes, don't say a fuckin' word—they do not exist. You did not see them, and that chopper was never fuckin' here, either," a sergeant would bark in a hoarse, gravelly voice that sounded like a heavy bag being thumped by Joe Frazier in February 1971, a month before he taught Muhammad Ali a lesson on boxing in beloved New York City, world capital of jazz, the city that never sleeps: Don't trade left hooks with a left-hooker.

Counterterrorists. As long as there are terrorists, there will be counterterrorists, whose sole reason for living is to roam the earth and kill terrorists. Killers, ghosts, dark-side ops warriors, spies, masters of the black arts.

Men who never forget that the first law of war is survival. You can take that to the bank; dig it hard and dig it good, that check will never bounce.

The Americans came to Iraq on July 10, 2002, to kill Al-Qaeda and take down Saddam with the help of the Kurds, who were highly motivated and truly inspired to end Saddam's dictatorship. When you lose 180,000 people to Saddam's chemical weapons and other massacres at Saddam's hands, as the Kurds did, it tends to focus one's attention.

When the American counterterrorists came, the Kurds were waiting with open arms in the ancient Kurdish town of Zakho, on the Turkish-Iraqi border, Kalashnikovs in hand, ready to help the counterterrorists take down Saddam and kill Al-Qaeda.

Some called the counterterrorists American samurai, because they were well skilled in the black arts, as the samurai were in ancient Japan. They were real-life James Bonds without British accents and Cambridge educations and martinis in casinos, but real-life James Bonds nonetheless—hard men who can work in any country as history professors or archeologists or gem dealers, and do, drop of a hat.

Counterterrorists—men who could disappear into a market in Cairo or a whorehouse in New Delhi or a bar in Lisbon, take care of business, and then fall away like a ghost in the night without a trace; men who had taken down Al-Qaeda terrorist cells on a shoestring, and among them, men who had heard Osama bin Laden on radio intercepts in Tora Bora, Afghanistan, calling for Al-Qaeda to retreat to safe havens in Pakistan in December 2001.

They were counterterrorists, and they had come to the Near East, not to order martinis or tell jokes about what is shaken or stirred, nor to inquire about topless women on European beaches; no, they had come to kill terrorists and end Saddam's dictatorship.

They were for-real counterterrorists, and this was a real, live counterterrorist operation against real, live Al-Qaeda terrorists in the Near East, the cultural and historic homeland of Al-Qaeda and all Islamist terrorism.

Now it was July 10, 2002, and the counterterrorists were crossing the Turkish border into Iraq. President George W. Bush had ordered them to carry out the operation. They all spoke conversational Kurdish and Arabic, and over half the team was fluent in Arabic.

All spoke the languages of hand-to-hand killing and knife fighting, and all were fluent in small arms.

All of them were prior-service U.S. military, combat arms, active duty, and all of them had survived, proving they were in line when God was handing out common sense.

They knew how to speak languages other than English, but they also knew how to kill better than they knew any foreign tongue.

If they got stamped by Al-Qaeda, if they got shot down or stabbed or beheaded, no director would yell, "Cut—that's a wrap. Let's go tap a keg." None of them came to Iraq to get stamped by Al-Qaeda or by Saddam's secret police. The counterterrorists came to Iraq well armed. They carried far more weapons than James Bond would ever carry because they were real killers, and they had come to kill terrorists and Saddam's secret police.

The counterterrorists never hesitated to kill terrorists because, as a British counterterrorist once said, "He who hesitates to kill terrorists is soon killed by terrorists. That is a true law of counterterrorism, and if you refuse to enforce that law, you die and the terrorist lives. Killing terrorists saves lives, and I am in business to save lives. I do not sell stocks and bonds, I am not an investment banker, and I do not sell life insurance. I am a counterterrorist and I kill terrorists for a living. This is what I do, what I enjoy, and I am damned good at it or else I wouldn't be doing it."

The counterterrorists had tracked and taken down terrorists on all lands and seas. The most senior of them, Charles S. Faddis—"Sam"—had been tracking terrorists for nearly twenty years by that summer of 2002. He had journeyed throughout the Near East, Europe, and South Asia in his career as a counterterrorist and CIA case officer. Well versed in the languages and cultures of the Near East, Sam and his counterterrorist team aimed to kill Al-Qaeda in Iraq and take down Saddam, ten months after Al-Qaeda's assault on the

American homeland. Fluent in the ways of the Mediterranean, he retired from the CIA in May 2008.

Eight together, the counterterrorists rolled over a concrete bridge into Iraq, driving jeeps alongside the dark, glittering waters of the Harburr River, which snakes like a belly dancer's hips and runs southeast through wheat fields and grape orchards and orange groves toward the high, dark rocky walls of the Zagros and Gara mountains of Kurdistan. They entered the land where people stopped speaking Turkish and started speaking Kurdish. The mountain ranges there, massive peaks that Kurdish *peshmerga* seized and held in the victorious forty-two-year Kurdish guerrilla war against Iraq, 1961–2003, have not changed since 10,000 years BC, like vast parts of Iraq.

The American counterterrorists had all volunteered for the clandestine operation to take place behind enemy lines in Iraq. A former U.S. Army armor officer, Sam commanded the counterterrorists in Kurdistan and Northern Iraq from July 2002 to May 2003. Six-foot two, broad-shouldered, gray-haired and silver-bearded, Sam was forty-seven years old that summer. He comes from the Appalachian Mountains of western Pennsylvania, and makes an impression with his dark eyes and calm, reflective manner. He speaks fluent Greek and Turkish, has a conversational proficiency in many Near Eastern languages, and holds both a bachelor's degree in political science and a law degree. His bookshelves are lined with works of history, fiction, and the poetry of Yeats, Homer, Dante, and Shakespeare.

Quiet, self-contained, possessing a wicked wit at times, he is but one type of counterterrorist, in a profession where the personalities range from Falstaffian, hail-fellow-well-met raconteurs to stand-up family men who easily pass for stockbrokers, and do, to masters of self-deprecatory understated humor who appear at first glance to be running fishing boats for a living in the Adriatic Sea but, in truth, are indeed hunting for sharks—sharks of a different sort, called terrorists.

A friend of mine, an Australian counterterrorist whom I'll call Odysseus for the purposes of this book, provides insight into the makeup of some counterterrorists—although, in truth, many counterterrorists are rock-solid, easygoing family men, low-key and dependable as the next sunrise, and look no different than a lawyer on M Street in Washington, or a hunting guide in the Pyrenees of Spain (as the situation requires). Odysseus, however, is a rogue, speaks five languages fluently, and enjoys the company of Spanish models and Russian actresses, rides a vintage 1968 Triumph motorcycle he imported from London (or drives his fully restored classic 1963 Porsche 356C), skydives, and holds a third-degree black belt in Shorin-Ryu karate and a first-degree black belt in Aikido.

A battered, dark-brown leather, custom-made 250-pound heavy bag hangs from a steel chain slung over a steel beam in the basement of his beach house on the southern coast of Australia. When not on missions, each morning at dawn Odysseus pulls on a rubber sauna suit, tosses gray sweats over the sauna suit, tugs on leather punching gloves with the fingertips cut off, and throws elbows, jabs, hooks, uppercuts, and crosses at the heavy bag for an hour. Then he jogs for an hour, religiously. Like Sam and his team, he has taken down

Al-Qaeda and other Islamist terrorists in the heartland of Al-Qaeda: the Near East and Central Asia.

Sam handpicked the counterterrorists and clandestine officers for his team in early February of 2002, at CIA headquarters in Langley, Virginia. Nearly half of his team had been heavily engaged in the fight against Al-Qaeda, the Taliban, and other Islamist terrorists in Afghanistan after September 11th.

Throughout February 2002, Sam and his team got refresher training on counterterrorist raid training; all firearms training; survival training and languages training in Arabic, Farsi, Kurdish, and Turkish; and refresher courses on reconnaissance and surveillance, and calling in air strikes, artillery strikes, and other call-for-fire commands on field radios at war.

Locked and cocked and told by the White House in January 2002 that war in Iraq was imminent, Sam had his team ready to go to war in Iraq by early March of 2002, on schedule.

From March 2002 to July 4, 2002, the Turkish General Staff gave on-again, off-again messages to the White House, until Sam told his superiors to relay the following to the Oval Office: "This administration gets stay-out-of-jail cards for my team; no more airport hopscotch for my men."

Even when they were en route to Iraq in July 2002, the Turkish General Staff ordered the counterterrorists not to land at the U.S. Air Force Base in Incirlik, Turkey. They landed, nonetheless, on July 7, 2002.

Three days later, each American carried an assault rifle and a sidearm into Kurdistan, clips jacked in and full magazines and ammunition stacked in the rear of their jeeps as they rolled across the river to link up with Kurdish *peshmerga*.

TRACKING AL-QAEDA, SADDAM, AND WMD

Kurdistan, July–August 2002

The counterterrorists blazed a dusty trail south to the Iranian border, after first meeting with Kurdish Democratic Party president Massoud Barzani and Barzani's inner circle in Salahuddin, central Kurdistan, on July 11, 2002. Land mines dotted the countryside, the land mines that Saddam's Iraqi Army had spread throughout Kurdistan with cold, ruthless precision— land mines that are still killing Kurdish children and farmers and shepherds in the fall of 2008. The counterterrorists rolled on, passing through fields posted with red skulls and crossbones, the international warning sign for land mines.

Three days later, on July 14, 2002, Sam and his counterterrorists had Al-Qaeda in their sights—a once-in-a-lifetime opportunity to strike and kill roughly a thousand Al-Qaeda terrorists and Ansar al-Islam terrorists.

Less than a year after September 11th, the chance to take down Al-Qaeda and Ansar al-Islam came directly from the counterterrorists' tight relationship with the Kurds.

As Sam said, "The Kurds never betrayed us. They were the best friends and comrades we had; we never could have survived without them. The Kurds took damn good care of us and they never hesitated to go in harm's way to take down Al-Qaeda.

1

True men of honor and courage." The Kurds embraced the counterterrorists like brothers. Respect is a two-way street, and the Kurds and Americans in-country lived that adage.

Throughout the boiling hot July in Iraq, missing the company of naked women and brandy, the counterterrorists targeted many terrorists—one thousand Islamist terrorists, to be exact—thanks to the Kurds. They had both Al-Qaeda and Ansar al-Islam terrorists in their gun sights. Al-Qaeda had built a chemical weapons factory near the Iranian border in far southern Kurdistan, the terrorist forts more like medieval castles than anything else. By August 2002, the counterterrorists had built solid human intelligence networks with the Kurds, and had the juice on Al-Qaeda, specifically: They were developing chemical and biological weapons at the Khurmal complex on the Iranian border.

The Kurds had turned over every stone and pebble in the rugged, rocky mountains of the Gara and Zagros ranges, deep in Kurdistan, to help the counterterrorists take down Al-Qaeda and Ansar al-Islam, and, of course, to help the counterterrorists track Saddam's secret police.

Throughout July, the counterterrorists apprised the White House of the existence of two hundred Al-Qaeda terrorists, and over seven hundred Ansar al-Islam terrorists, which included the entire senior leadership of Ansar al-Islam.

The White House response: *Duly noted.*

Khurmal was loaded with Al-Qaeda terrorists who'd escaped from Tora Bora in December 2001, regrouping—and rearming—on the Iranian border. The Kurds were already dying in July and August of 2002 for the American cause of taking down Saddam and Al-Qaeda. The counterterrorists mourned the loss of their Kurdish comrades and carried on, taking the fight to Al-Qaeda in Iraq. There, they lost some of their Kurdish spies, who'd been captured, tortured, and killed by Al-Qaeda, Ansar al-Islam, and Saddam's *Mukhabarat* secret police.

Al-Qaeda's methods of torture in Iraq were as medieval as their architecture.

Kurdish spies were brutally tormented, their bodies dismembered by Al-Qaeda, Ansar al-Islam, and the *Mukhabarat*. The Kurds were disemboweled, quartered, and beheaded, their heads stuck on pikes for ravens to feast on along the Iranian border.

Al-Qaeda was lashed up with Ansar al-Islam near the Iranian border, in the remote highlands where Persian warriors under Xerxes' command once marched on their way to meeting Spartan swords at Thermopylae in 480 BC. King Leonidas and his Spartan warriors crushed thousands and thousands of Persians before the Spartans' last stand on the third day of battle, taking on wave after wave of Persians to defend the freedom of all Greece in a battle that changed the course of history, immortalized in the lines of Simonides, Greek poet and historian:

Go tell the Spartans, passerby
That here, obedient to their laws, we lie.

The counterterrorists, true Spartans to the core—although unlike the Spartans, they enjoyed modern-day pleasures, such as premium Kentucky bourbon—had discovered in Northern Iraq that a thousand Islamist terrorists had made a home along the Iranian border in heavily fortified positions with massive, three- to four-foot-thick walls made of concrete, stone, mortar, and brick.

Sam and the counterterrorists remained bore-sighted on taking down Al-Qaeda and Ansar al-Islam, eleven months after September 11th.

Sam recalls:

We had reports from the Kurds that Al-Qaeda terrorists were lashed up with Ansar al-Islam terrorists, and developing chemical and biological weapons at the Khurmal facility.

In fact, the facility was at a village named Sargat, not far from Khurmal. Our job was to figure out what's going on with this chemical stuff, what's going on with the biological stuff. Nasty stuff, deadly like nobody's business.

We had to investigate, get hard intelligence on the chemical and biological weapons, nail down actual numbers of Al-Qaeda and Ansar al-Islam. Investigate, get hard intelligence, verify and confirm.

Turned out that our initial field intelligence on Al-Qaeda developing chemical and biological weapons at Khurmal, Intel from Kurdish sources, was not bogus.

First thing we did was talk with Patriotic Union of Kurdistan (PUK) *peshmerga.* We sent people out and got them right up on the line, as close to Ansar al-Islam and Al-Qaeda as we could. Making direct observation and mapping the turf.

A counterterrorist must never rely solely on technical intelligence, but must use his own eyeballs to take down a terrorist.

We got eyes on Al-Qaeda and Ansar al-Islam heavy-machine-gun positions, mortar sites, and those damned medieval-style castles.

We carried out all our reconnaissance and surveillance in *peshmerga* clothes, carrying *peshmerga* weapons. We kept eyes on Al-Qaeda and Ansar al-Islam throughout July, going into August 2002, marking terrorist positions, marking all their machine-gun posts, every position that we could get eyes on and nail down exact, precise grid coordinates.

The Kurdish *peshmerga* tended to give us rather exotic descriptions of the terrorist positions, such as "It's near where my mother's goat gave birth in the year of the heavy snow, before I learned how to play guitar in my dissolute youth, in a time of thunder and lightning." Which doesn't translate well on a field radio. But together, we nailed the terrorists' locations.

Our people were really far out, and within range of Al-Qaeda and Ansar al-Islam. I mean, damn close—you could see their fortified positions with the naked eye, easily. You could see the color of their *khaffiyahs*.

Next thing we discovered was that Kurdish *peshmerga* had actually captured Al-Qaeda and Ansar al-Islam. We got names off them; the *peshmerga* had tried questioning them, but had made no significant progress on the interrogations. We waded in, began interrogating at least two dozen. We determined that the Kurds were telling the truth about Al-Qaeda being there, and also, the Kurds were not aware of just how many Al-Qaeda they had in custody.

The Kurds were not exaggerating; the Patriotic Union of Kurdistan had, unknowingly, significantly underestimated the extent of Al-Qaeda's penetration into Northern Iraq. What we discovered here was that there were two hundred Al-Qaeda terrorists who'd escaped the dragnet in Tora Bora in December 2001, made it across Iran, and were now in Ansar al-Islam territory. We also discovered that Al-Qaeda had an existing relationship with Ansar al-Islam. Prior to losing their operational bases in Afghanistan, Al-Qaeda had discussed countries to penetrate where new bases could be established, with new Islamist terrorist allies; Ansar al-Islam in Northern Iraq was one of them. The relationship between Al-Qaeda and Ansar al-Islam in Northern Iraq was very much the same as the relationship between Al-Qaeda and the Taliban in Afghanistan.

I remember thinking, as we got into this, "This is like a virus. It just replicates itself. Al-Qaeda had showed up, with money, and bought themselves a safe haven, established presence, linked up and built cells.

Which is exactly what they'd done with the Taliban in Afghanistan, from 1996 on.

It's like a monster that you cut up into many pieces, but the pieces just drift elsewhere and replicate that same monster.

And the vast majority of people fighting this war against Islamist terrorism, globally, are Muslims. That is not an issue for the media, but a reality of our time, and very real for all Muslims.

Muslims are suffering from Islamist terrorism like nobody else. Don't get me wrong: I know for a fact that Islamist terrorists are fully committed to destroying Israel and the West, no question about it. But Islamist terrorism has the potential to destroy Islam, which would be catastrophic for Muslims, and a great loss for humanity.

For every American killed by Al-Qaeda and other Islamist terrorists since February 26, 1993, Al-Qaeda's first act of war against the United States, at least one hundred Muslims have died fighting the same enemy we are fighting. The only reason we were able to accomplish our missions in Kurdistan was because of our Muslim ally, the Kurds.

Other things we determined in July 2002, just rolling, operational around the clock, 24/7 (we never closed): We discovered chemical/biological activity, real, verified chemical and biological weapons activity, in Sargat. Al-Qaeda and Ansar al-Islam were doing a lot of work in Sargat, near Khurmal, trying to create chemical and biological agents, different types of gas—chemical agents for assassinations, and to poison people; chemical and biological agents to put on a door handle in a public place, like seats and doors in a railroad car. The poisons were contact poisons, to create death once anyone touched a door handle, railway car window, and so on.

Al-Qaeda and Ansar al-Islam were also developing different types of chemical gas to put in ventila-
tion systems for mass casualties, biological agents.
Some of it was rudimentary, but the majority of it
was going on with a lot of effort. They were full-
bore on chemical and biological warfare at Sargat. It
was clear that Sargat was dedicated to Al-Qaeda's
chemical and biological weapons research. They
were doing a lot of testing on donkeys, rabbits, mice,
and other animals.

That was all very, very troubling. The problem
is that once Al-Qaeda dedicates a facility to this, it
is not too damn difficult at all to create chemical
and biological weapons. People exaggerate the dif-
ficulty of creating chemical agents for warfare. A
lot of chemical and biological warfare dates back
to the late 1800s, and a lot of it is basic chemistry.
All of the information is available widely, all around
the planet.

Al-Qaeda and Ansar al-Islam had their hands on
large stockpiles of cyanide at Sargat, which is available all over the Near East in the metallurgy business. Cyanide is not a controlled substance; anyone
can transport it, anywhere. Al-Qaeda and Ansar al-
Islam were ordering large truckloads of cyanide and
having it shipped and delivered to Sargat. They were
experimenting with using it as a contact poison—
in food, for instance; they were exploring different
ways to disperse it, to form a cyanide gas, which
could be used in a subway car, railway car, or any
other large confined space, like a movie theater.

All you need is the Internet and time, to know how to make those attacks. We conducted inter-rogations of Al-Qaeda terrorists, held by the PUK *peshmerga*, near Sargat.

Every Al-Qaeda terrorist that Sam questioned, and all the Ansar al-Islam terrorists that he and his counterterrorists also questioned, ended up talking. Their conversations basically went like this: "I have no idea why I am here. You think I am a terrorist? Oh no; I was just standing on a mountain, read-ing my Koran, and these mean Kurdish men (who are not true Muslims) grabbed me from the beautiful land, where the mountain skies are forever peaceful and there is happiness, joy, and a state of perpetual bliss, and here I am. Please let me go and tell the mean Kurdish men to please go away."

The Al-Qaeda terrorists were from all across the Near East: Jordanians, Syrians, Sunni Arab Iraqis, and Kurds. They'd escaped from Tora Bora and other areas of Afghani-stan in early December 2001.

Seven months after Gary Berntsen, a veteran CIA counter-terrorism officer and a longtime comrade of Sam Faddis, had pleaded for U.S. Army Rangers at Tora Bora in late November and early December 2001, urging the White House to strike and kill many of these same Al-Qaeda terrorists, Al-Qaeda was already rebuilding with Ansar al-Islam in Northern Iraq in July 2002. Their chemical and biological warfare base was blossom-ing, and their financial network was clicking on all gears.

While interrogating the many Islamist terrorists that his team and the Kurds had captured in the summer of 2002,

Sam and the counterterrorists saw no virtue in torturing terrorists:

> Nobody ever laid a finger on any terrorists we cap-
> tured, in my team's interrogations. Nobody slapped
> them around; nobody so much as touched them. You
> can't interrogate people and get information out of
> them if you are out of control. If you hurt people
> that you are trying to get information out of, they
> will only lie to you, or feed you some variation of a
> lie, which at the end of the day gets you nowhere
> near the truth. I was always told in the U.S. Army, as
> you were told as a Marine, "If you are captured and
> tortured, feed some misinformation to stop the tor-
> ture; don't hesitate to lie."

Now, in early August 2002, Sam nailed down the fact that there were not several dozen Al-Qaeda terrorists lashed up with Ansar al-Islam, but several *hundred* of them, all escaped from Afghanistan. He immediately sent that field intelligence to Washington. The White House response: *Duly noted.*

Together with the counterterrorists, Sam plowed ahead, going into early August 2002, interrogating captured Islamist terrorists. They were fed and sheltered, and the counterterrorists broke them down psychologically, over a period of weeks. The terrorists had no idea why they were there. It was more of the same—the "joy and bliss on a mountain with my Koran and my sheep and goats, but the evil Kurds, who are not true Muslims, kidnapped me" routine. The Kurds were not amused by the terrorists' remarks regarding the purity of their faith.

Then, after a few days of interrogations, Al-Qaeda began singing a different tune. At the beginning, it was: "I was in Afghanistan, sure, but purely for religious reasons." At the end of the week, that changed to: "Well, I *am* sympathetic to Al-Qaeda. But while I agree with Osama bin Laden on certain issues, and share some of their beliefs, I am not really Al-Qaeda." In the second week of interrogations, that changed to: "Yes, I am Al-Qaeda. I love Osama bin Laden, and I was at Tora Bora. The Taliban are my brothers, and I smiled when the World Trade Center disappeared on September 11th."

The Al-Qaeda terrorists in Iraq gave up exact, specific details on Tora Bora in Afghanistan—mountain passes and trails, for instance. The counterterrorists' basic line with them was, "Look, dude, if you don't consider yourself of value to us, then we'll just leave you to the care and comfort of the Patriotic Union of Kurdistan, and you'll just rot in Kurdistan for the rest of your natural-born days."

Sam went on:

"What's your wife's plan, for when you never come back?" we'd ask. Man, they never had an answer to that. And we'd ask them, "Look, how are your sons going to be raised, without a father? How is your wife going to feed herself? Your sons and daughters are going to grow up without a father and with no idea of what happened to you."

I will never forget one kid we interviewed, in particular; this was late July 2002. Eighteen years old, Kurdish kid—just a squeaky-clean, really young-looking kid. He'd be a high school senior, stateside. Ansar al-Islam had convinced him to become a suicide bomber in early July 2002; they had put a suicide vest on him and sent him to blow up a police station in Kurdistan, near Halapja. His suicide bomb was hidden under a ski jacket, and it was six 82mm mortar rounds hard-wired to a cable with a switch that would go off in his pocket, a thumb switch.

His instructions from his Ansar al-Islam suicide bomb cadre were: "You've got to get inside and up the stairs. Just tell them you were robbed and you want to talk to a cop. Press the switch with your thumb, and you'll be in the arms of the blessed virgin girls, in Paradise for all eternity."

The kid walks up to the police station, just shuffling forward, and a cop outside stops him and says, "Hey, what do you have in your pocket?"

"I have the switch to my suicide vest in my pocket," the kid said.

The cop, not missing a beat, said, "How about you take your hands out of your pockets, then, nice and easy." So the kid took his hands out of his pockets and all hell broke loose, and they hustled him inside.

I looked at the kid. I asked him, "Why did you do that?"

The kid told us, "I just thought about it, and I thought, 'I'd rather not die today.'" We got him a Coke. And another counterterrorist said to him, "That was a good idea, man. You're not even legal yet. You need to find a beer and a girlfriend."

The kid smiled and said, "That sounds like a good idea."

Looking into his eyes, you could tell he'd reckoned that getting busy living is a damn sight more exciting than getting busy dying. He then told Sam that for the first time in his life, he'd realized that it's the Islamist imams who are always recruiting young Muslim men who have never been with a woman to wear the suicide vests, but none of the Islamist imams were wearing the suicide vests. The young man was now fascinated by this insight, and said, "It is now in the front of my mind, in my waking hours."

Fortunately, the suicide bomber had realized that the Islamist imams who were preaching that death is a road to eternal bliss were certainly sleeping with Muslim virgin women, right here on earth. The men preaching to the kid that he needed to die in order to enjoy the pleasure of a woman's company were not strapping on the suicide vests, and they had not pitched this to him in some abstract way. Nobody said to him, "You'll be at one with God." No, they'd told him, "You'll press the switch and then you'll be in an orgy with beautiful Muslim virgin women, for eternity."

Now, you're eighteen, you've never been with a woman, and after you press the suicide switch, you're in the Eternal Orgy where the virgins all look like Miss Universe, sex never ends, and all *jihad* ends in bliss. Strangely enough, the Assassins preached the same message to their Islamist terrorists before their suicide missions, nine hundred years ago in the Near East. No one ever thought to inform the young men of the Assassins, or their spiritual, cultural, and religious descendants, the young men of Islamist terrorism in our time, that heaven is being in a woman's arms right here on earth.

The Islamist imams also put incredible pressure on this kid's family, and he told Sam and the counterterrorists, "The imams jabbed their fingers in the air in the days before my suicide mission, jumping around, screaming, 'Your family needs the money, and you must get them the money, in this way. Don't worry, paradise is your reward!'" The kid was from a poor family, like many suicide bombers, and the money handed his parents after his death would fill rice bowls that normally went empty. The imams know this, when they pressure Muslim youth to strap on the suicide vest, just as that imam did with that Kurdish kid.

At the end of the day, the kid was very lucky that the Kurdish cop near Halapja didn't put two rounds in his head when he told the cop that he had his hand on the switch in his pocket. By international procedure, that's what you do to suicide bombers.

Sam had Kurdish spies throughout Ansar al-Islam territory by mid-August 2002, reporting daily, in great detail, on Al-Qaeda and Ansar al-Islam terrorists, and the chemical and biological weapons being developed by Al-Qaeda at Sargat, near Khurmal.

The Americans had followed one of the key ancient laws of clandestine operations and war—build and maintain a broad, deep human intelligence network—with great effectiveness in Kurdistan during the summer of 2002.

Sam's main counterterrorist operations chieftain was taking all the field intelligence from the Kurds and, furthermore, putting it into a plan to take down Al-Qaeda, their chemical/biological warfare center at Sargat, and Ansar al-Islam—lock, stock, and many smoking mortar tubes. The Kurds took pictures of Al-Qaeda and Ansar al-Islam machine-gun positions and mortar sites, and also, crucial to the planned assault on Al-Qaeda/Ansar al-Islam, got global positioning system ten-digit coordinates on every terrorist position (GPS ten-digit grids).

Five years later, in the fall of 2007, Sam laid out the planned assault on Al-Qaeda/Ansar al-Islam, in full. We were sitting among an international crowd in a jazz club in Washington, D.C., with Michael Brecker playing "Pilgrimage" out of the speakers on a late October afternoon. Irish whiskey in hand, Sam recounted the plan:

> Obviously, we had imagery of all these locations that we matched up with our own field intelligence. What we ended up with was photographs and ten-digit grids of every enemy position—all the compounds for every Al-Qaeda terrorist and all of the Ansar al-Islam leadership.
>
> We knew exactly where every one of these one thousand Islamist terrorists slept. And we knew where each gun was, literally down to every machine-gun position and mortar tube.
>
> Max, who was my operations guru, an exceptional mind for all matters operational, pulled together an

operational plan to go in, right then, in the second week of August 2002.

By this point, we'd sent thousands of intelligence reports back to headquarters. Headquarters was psyched; they were stoked. It was like you had a candle in the middle of a room, and now they were seeing floodlights in the same space. They went from glimmers to pure clarity.

However, the White House refused to give us the green light to take down over two hundred Al-Qaeda, the Al-Qaeda chemical and biological warfare center at Sargat, and over seven hundred Ansar al-Islam terrorists, which of course included the entire leadership of Ansar al-Islam.

And none of the terrorists knew we had them in our sights; none of them knew we were there. Stealth and surprise were completely on our side.

Max pulled together a detailed military plan for attacking the enemy enclave. This was a plan to overrun and occupy the enclave, and to destroy all of Al-Qaeda/Ansar al-Islam terrorists.

All the Al-Qaeda terrorists had escaped from Afghanistan.

It was obvious from the outset that one of the dangers was going to be the possibility that most of the key guys we wanted had an escape route into safe haven in Iran. The enclave was right on the Iranian border. This was all east of Halapja.

Some of the locations, particularly where Al-Qaeda was located at Biyara, were up at high elevation, and almost right dead smack on the border.

This was extremely remote, mountainous terrain, no major roads of any kind. Anybody could see that if you wanted to take the bastards down, you'd have to block the border.

Max was to lead the main force, only possible with total stealth, which we had in full.

The plan was to take our guys deep with Delta Force and SEAL Team Six, clandestine, and get on the border behind Al-Qaeda and Ansar al-Islam, and then launch the main assault with PUK, using all our field Intel. That way, once we went in and drove them, we'd get them all. They could either die or surrender.

The key factor was that Ansar al-Islam had a whole series of fortified positions, lashed up with Al-Qaeda. Nobody on either side had any artillery. Tactically, there was a medieval quality to the way Ansar al-Islam fought. Ansar al-Islam built fortified positions, very medieval, and defended them, because the modern weapons needed to destroy a castle and prevent a siege from happening in the first place—like fighter jets, bombers, and artillery—did not exist in the area.

Now, a real advantage we had was that the Patriotic Union of Kurdistan *peshmerga* had a fair number of 120mm mortar tubes, from the Soviets, but very limited stocks of ammunition. A formidable weapon in mountain warfare, and fine for our assault plan, if the U.S. military could not show up to kill Al-Qaeda.

Given what had happened at Tora Bora in December 2001, when the White House did not order U.S.

military to kill Al-Qaeda and Osama bin Laden, we had to plan, of course, for the White House not to give us air support, or any other U.S. military support, to kill Al-Qaeda and Ansar al-Islam terrorists in Iraq.

Now, the Patriotic Union of Kurdistan did have a few hundred 120mm mortar rounds, but keep in mind that the PUK had to balance their concerns of using those few 120mm mortar rounds to defend against Saddam, and also with their ongoing, knock-down drag-out guerrilla war against Ansar al-Islam and their Islamist terrorist allies, including Al-Qaeda, of course.

And the PUK, like the Kurdish Democratic Party, knew that the White House had kept none of their promises to the Kurds in the summer of 2002, regarding weapons, ammunition, and supplies. So, the Kurds had to be real careful. In any event, the PUK's limited 120mm mortar stocks were not going to be sufficient for the assault on Al-Qaeda and Ansar al-Islam.

Vital to our operations in Kurdistan and Northern Iraq were two counterterrorists who were on the team that took Kabul, after September 11th—the team that Schroen took in, and then Gary Berntsen, who commanded that team and led them to Tora Bora. One of my counterterrorists was in Tora Bora and confirmed everything that Gary Berntsen said in *Jawbreaker:* "Let's finish this now. Let's kill all these bastards."

He and Gary Berntsen remain convinced to this day that we could have finished taking down

Al-Qaeda, right there, right then—including Osama bin Laden.

Gary had guys calling in fire in Tora Bora, from hills and ravines and mountaintops, and Gary and his team were listening on radio intercepts to Osama bin Laden giving his farewell address to the Taliban and all jihadists in Afghanistan.

Late November to mid-December, 2001, Gary begged the White House and CIA headquarters for at least one battalion of U.S. Army Rangers to end it—to kill Osama bin Laden and strike and kill Al-Qaeda and Taliban in Tora Bora.

Well, Gary was being told from Langley, and it was the official U.S. government position, that Pakistan was sealing the border.

So, the White House never sent the Rangers, and the border remained porous. Gary saw on the ground in Tora Bora that Pakistan didn't seal a goddamn thing. This was the second congenital failure of the White House to take down Al-Qaeda.

The third was in Northern Iraq, less than a year later. First was spring 2001, of course; the White House really wanted that tax cut, but didn't want to kill Al-Qaeda. Meanwhile, the U.S. military didn't show in Tora Bora in December 2001, just like they didn't show for us in 2002.

With Al-Qaeda in our gun sights in northern Iraq in August 2002, we saw the same dynamic that Gary saw in Tora Bora in December 2001.

We were primed and ready to go against Al-Qaeda and Ansar al-Islam. One thousand Islamist terrorists in our gun sights, including the entire leadership of Ansar al-Islam. And our first option in August 2002 was to get U.S. military assistance, from U.S. Special Operations Command. Our first option was to get guys on the ground, Delta Force and SEAL Team Six. Rangers.

But CENTCOM wouldn't go for that. So, we'd reduce it to: "They won't put anybody on the ground—can we at least get air strikes?" All we'd really need, in that case, was two B-52s.

Since we had exact ten-digit grids, they'd enter that into the JDAM and the bombs. In the war, that's how we worked the intelligence and made the raids, in that fashion. Well, we asked for that, and we didn't get that, either.

And finally, we said, "Give us some 120mm mortar rounds and we'll do it ourselves." And that plan was also disapproved by CENTCOM and headquarters.

At the end of the day, Al-Qaeda and Ansar al-Islam walked.

It was clear that Al-Qaeda was reconstituting itself in Northern Iraq in August 2002. It was clear that Al-Qaeda had built a chemical/biological warfare center, in Sargat.

We had a golden opportunity to kill over two hundred Al-Qaeda and just crush and destroy Ansar al-Islam. And end it, right there and then.

Instead of letting these Al-Qaeda and Ansar al-Islam terrorists walk away, build more cells, expand their networks, and carry out more terrorist attacks.

U.S. Marine scout/sniper Corporal Dudley Kelso, from Tupelo, Mississippi, is absolutely right: "Dead terrorists build no cells. Dead terrorists open no offshore accounts. And dead terrorists do not kill Americans and our allies." Kelso is in the black; that is totally accurate.

The White House refused to give us any U.S. military support, to strike and kill Al-Qaeda and Ansar al-Islam, so we went to our backup plan: air-drop the 120mm mortar rounds.

I kept fighting to take down Al-Qaeda, but nothing changed from the White House.

Our premier U.S. military counterterrorism assets for taking down Al-Qaeda—Delta Force, SEAL Team Six, U.S. Army Rangers, and Marine Force Recon— were never given to my team, which is criminal, as we are at war with Al-Qaeda, and it was, of course, only eleven months after September 11th.

The SOCOM assets I requested are all well capable of clandestine missions, extraordinarily well trained in counterterrorism, and in the case of Delta Force and SEAL Team Six, specifically created to strike and kill terrorists.

But the White House decided that they wanted to let Al-Qaeda walk, give Ansar al-Islam a pass, and watch Al-Qaeda develop chemical and biological weapons of mass destruction in the Near East. I kept fighting, even though headquarters was telling me that there was no way the White House would let us punch Al-Qaeda's ticket.

Max came up with two final plans: One involved two B-52s; the other was without any air support whatsoever, simply a heavy mortar attack on Al-Qaeda/Ansar al-Islam, followed by an assault on their base—we would've surrounded their base, to begin with.

It came down to me saying to headquarters, "Okay, for the love of God, just give us two B-52s, or just the mortars, and we'll get it done. We've got every one of their gun positions and mortar sites zeroed in, ten-digit grids on every one of them. Give it to us tomorrow, and we'll get it done the day after. Al-Qaeda and Ansar al-Islam don't have a clue that we are here. Total stealth."

All we needed was five hundred 120mm mortar rounds, roughly two thousand Kalashnikovs, 50,000 7.62 rounds, and the green light to strike and kill a thousand Islamist terrorists and destroy their chemical/biological warfare center at Sargat.

To even get that in-country, however, we needed air assets, and remember—the Turks had denied us planes or choppers into Kurdistan in the first place, so getting the weapons and supplies to take down Al-Qaeda terrorists and Ansar al-Islam terrorists required Turkish permission.

Upon reflection, the White House had a decision to make: Strike and kill Al-Qaeda, with or without Turkish permission, or let Al-Qaeda walk and keep our NATO ally Turkey happy.

The White House decided against killing Al-Qaeda, obviously. Aside from my eight men, it would've been all Kurdish *peshmerga;* it was our op and our command, of course. The Kurds were incredibly motivated, absolutely sky-high to take down Al-Qaeda and Ansar al-Islam. No substitute for fighting spirit. Our fighting spirit was on par with the Kurds;

we were all there to take down Al-Qaeda, and we had the perfect opportunity to do exactly what our mission called for.

CIA headquarters relayed the White House order to Sam: *Let Al-Qaeda walk.*

The Kurds were dumbfounded, confused and at wit's end when the White House didn't pull the trigger on Al-Qaeda and Ansar a-Islam. Here Sam and the counterterrorists had climbed into the belly of the beast. The Kurds had risked everything to ally themselves with the American cause, to stand and fight with Sam and his men. Now, Sam was aware of suggestions, stateside, that Al-Qaeda was in bed with Saddam, and that both were more than a little pregnant. Al-Qaeda terrorists near the Iranian border were operating in an area not controlled by Saddam, however. And Saddam had no love for Ansar al-Islam.

Sam briefed his team: "You'll get people saying the moon is made of green cheese, Saddam is in bed with Osama bin Laden, and Al-Qaeda is eating goat meat and rice in back alleys in Mosul. Look, if we can produce solid intelligence that proves Saddam is in bed with Al-Qaeda, that's fabulous. But we're not saying anything remotely like that until we get solid evidence that's happening. We're not going to pass off rumors and bullshit as the truth."

What Sam did discover was that Iraqi intelligence was active in the area, and they were spying on Ansar al-Islam. The counterterrorists discovered that and identified their officers, Saddam's *Mukhabarat.* All of this was reported, in full detail, and reached the White House. There was no ambiguity in the counterterrorists' field intelligence. They never found anything that suggested Al-Qaeda was lashed up with Saddam's government.

The only American clandestine team in Iraq before the invasion, they also had a mission to search for Saddam's weapons of mass destruction.

Before going in-country, the counterterrorists had been told in Washington: "We know the Iraqis have chemical weapons." One of their main missions was to collect intelligence on these weapons.

It is indisputable that not only did the Americans think that Saddam had weapons of mass destruction, but the senior Iraqi military also believed, beyond a doubt, that Iraq had WMD. This complicated matters a great deal when it came to the counterterrorists' efforts to collect intelligence about these weapons. Say you've got a source, an Iraqi brigade commander, and you ask him, "Do you have chemical weapons?" Sam continued his tale:

He'd look us in the eye and he'd reply, "Absolutely— and I have been told we will use them." In some cases, he'd even present you with the written Iraqi doctrine which outlined exactly *how* they would use them. Well, that certainly makes it very complex, in terms of denying Saddam had WMD. We couldn't send clandestine field officers to search every haystack and sand dune in Iraq to prove a negative.

While Saddam was disarming to make the inspectors go away, he simultaneously wanted his enemies to believe that he was lying and that he still had weapons, to sow fear in his enemies—the Kurds, for instance, and the Iranians. Now, how are you going to disprove that Iraqi brigade commander? You'd have to go to every military base, every location in Iraq, and prove a negative.

When you think about it, it's a twisted situation. You have Saddam, who's been accused of possessing WMD, and he's largely divested himself of these things, and yet at the same time he is actively attempting to convince, at least his own people, that he *hasn't* divested himself of WMD in order to hold on to power.

Saddam always believed that he would be able to dodge out from under any attack. He was playing a dual game: simultaneously trying to convince the inspectors that he had dissolved his large stockpile—which he had—while also deliberately conveying the impression to his internal opposition and his enemies in the region that this was a sham, and that indeed, he still had WMD.

It's really a twisted logic, when you reflect on it, but that was how Saddam's mind worked.

It apparently never occurred to him that by deliberately conveying the impression that he still had WMD, it would strengthen the U.S. case for taking him down.

Saddam sealed his own fate. Because his deception was so pervasive within his own security structure and military, and because the vast majority of his people believed Saddam's deception, we could recruit spies all day long throughout Iraq and every single one of them would tell us, "I believe and understand that Saddam has WMD, and he is going to use them." They couldn't lead us to the weapons; they couldn't give us samples; but from the most senior levels on down, the Iraqis in Saddam's government told us, "Absolutely, we have WMD, and absolutely we will use these weapons in the event of an invasion."

I never talked to a single Iraqi asset who had any question or doubt whatsoever about WMD—nobody believed that Saddam had gotten rid of these weapons.

However, we never reported to Washington that we'd found any WMD, because we never did. After all the work we did, we never said we'd found any sarin, mustard gas, nuclear weapons, or any other WMD.

The White House was making the case for Saddam having weapons of mass destruction while we were the only CIA operation on the ground in Iraq, collecting intelligence on Saddam and WMD. I'd tell my team, "Hey, dudes, we've been here a helluva long time on the ground, and we haven't picked up a single existing asset in the entire country, and so who is providing the information to Bush that is so rock-solid on weapons of mass destruction?"

We never provided it. We never found a stockpile. We couldn't find a smoking gun.

We never told the White House that the CIA had determined that Saddam had weapons of mass destruction, because we never determined that on the ground in Iraq.

So when George Tenet famously told Bush, regarding WMD, "It's a slam-dunk," I have no idea where Tenet was coming from, because I know for a fact that my team was the only clandestine U.S. asset in Iraq before Bush dispatched Colin Powell to New York to make the case for Saddam having weapons of mass destruction. We never reported WMD to CIA headquarters.

The other key mission in Salahuddin in late August 2002 was talking to the *peshmerga* on the Green Line, and meeting the *peshmerga* who would be on the tip of the spear in Northern Iraq, to strike and kill the Iraqi Army and all of Saddam's secret police. Sam often met with General Nawshirwan Mustafa Amin, a top Kurdish Democratic Party *peshmerga* general and the commander for that sector of the Green Line.

Sam described General Amin as "very savvy, clever, and tough. A totally no-bullshit guy. One of the most impressive combat commanders, anywhere, I have ever met."

General Amin commanded in the Erbil sector, vital to all Kurdistan. This was the first time in six years that the U.S. had laid eyes on that area. The American counterterrorists and clandestine field officers were keen on the readiness of KDP *peshmerga,* disposition of forces, fighting spirit, weapons, and ammunition. The counterterrorists journeyed to a number of different KDP positions on the Green Line, in just a couple of days, in late August 2002.

"The *peshmerga* were great, as always," Sam said. "They were pumped, and obviously eager to hear that we were going to get rid of Saddam."

South of Erbil, the *peshmerga* positions were a long damn way from the mountains. The land is flat as far as the eye can see.

You could see the Iraqi Army positions, just a few kilometers away. Tanks, artillery, rockets, and mechanized infantry. Choppers. Jets.

Now, the *peshmerga* had light infantry and gun trucks. Sam and the counterterrorists were well forward, and many times, they were within small-arms range of Iraqi Army units on the Green Line. Of course, the Iraqis were also looking at the Americans, who were dressed as *peshmerga*.

It was perfect terrain for armored warfare. And a real thin line of lightly armed Kurdish *peshmerga* with nothing heavier than RPGs stood between the Americans and the Iraqi Army. RPGs only work against gun trucks and light armored vehicles, but don't do a damn thing against a T-72.

Sam asked General Amin: "What's the plan should Saddam cross the Green Line with armor, artillery, and infantry?"

"The plan is to retreat to the hills," the *peshmerga* general replied. "We're face-to-face with 150,000 Iraqi troops. They've got tanks, surface-to-surface missiles, jet fighters, helicopters, and artillery. We've got Kalashnikovs and RPGs and our balls. We will beat them in the mountains, like before. We'll fight in the hills and use the high ground against them."

Sam realized that the Kurds had a major city, Erbil, right in the middle of all this. If the Iraqis advanced even a short distance, that entire city was going to come within artillery range of the Iraqi Army.

And you had hundreds of thousands of people who were going to be in a free-fire zone when this kicked off, if the Iraqis wanted to light it up. Erbil was already in surface-to-surface missile range of the Iraqi Army, and the Kurds kept drumming that into the heads of the counterterrorists who were on the Green Line.

The White House, however, provided no plan to save Erbil, despite countless messages that the counterterrorists sent to CIA headquarters for the White House, requesting that they be allowed to move decisively on a plan to save Erbil and other Kurdish towns and cities from chemical death.

Saddam had used chemical weapons of mass destruction on the Kurds many times before, and Sam had no doubt he'd wage chemical warfare on the Kurds again. The Kurds understood that; Sam understood that; the counterterrorists understood that; but the White House did not.

Sam and the counterterrorists had to assume that the Iraqis could put chemical warheads on their missiles and cause tens of thousands of deaths, hundreds of thousands of deaths. Saddam had certainly done it before.

The Iraqis also had the capacity to put nerve gas into Erbil anytime they wanted. In Sam's first meeting with General Amin, within minutes, the *peshmerga* general asked the counterterrorist commander, "How are we going to protect Erbil?" meaning, "What are *you* going to do about it?" And this was coming from a man who had personally experienced the horrific reality of chemical warfare on Kurdish soil.

Each day, General Amin said to the counterterrorists on the Green Line, "This is all terrific, that you are going to take down Saddam, but what is Bush's plan? How is Bush planning to protect Erbil? How is Bush going to stop Saddam from killing the people of Kurdistan with chemical weapons, yet again?"

Sam and a counterterrorist, fluent in many dialects of Arabic and Kurdish, sat cross-legged on carpets in a bare-bones courtyard of a *peshmerga* base in Erbil in late August, talking at length with General Amin about ending Saddam's regime. Sam recalls:

> I could see in his eyes that he was thinking, "I've got the Devil, Saddam Hussein, right in my backyard, and I haven't seen anything yet that tells me the White House has a plan to take him down."
>
> You could see he was thinking, "All I really know is that Bush listens closely to Henry Kissinger, who abandoned us in 1975, and Bush's father is George H. W. Bush, who abandoned us in 1991."
>
> I kept telling Mustafa, "You've gotta trust me—this is going to happen," doing everything I could to establish credibility with the Kurds and hoping that I could cash those checks.
>
> But I never told the Kurds that everything in our own communications system was telling us that Washington was completely divorced from reality.
>
> Of course, Mustafa was talking to us about chemical weapons—and that issue with chemical weapons reverberated throughout the entire deployment; the closer we got to the war, the bigger it got—and there was no doubt in anybody's mind that Saddam

was in possession of chemical weapons and that he would use them.

I was meeting every day with *peshmerga* who'd survived many Iraqi Army chemical attacks, who knew Iraqi brutality as a way of life, and who knew, personally, that Saddam would use chemical weapons on towns and cities because he'd never hesitated to use them before.

All Sam could tell General Amin was the damn sad truth: that the White House had no plan to stop Saddam's surface-to-surface missiles, nor chemical weapons.

With the counterterrorists, meanwhile, Sam had worked the problem of Saddam using chemical weapons on the Kurds, and the counterterrorists came up with an idea: buy gas masks and issue them to the Kurds, en masse. Just put out a contract and buy several hundred thousand gas masks, and as a gesture of good faith, give them to the Kurds. Washington blew that off. Said it was too expensive. It was cheaper, according to Washington, just to let the Kurds die in chemical attacks.

When Sam and the counterterrorists got closer to the invasion, they created their own solution, together with the Kurds.

The Americans and Kurds manned teams together to go behind Iraqi lines and destroy Saddam's surface-to-surface missiles.

The other wild card, or rogue pawn, as it were, is that the Kurds were explicitly told in February 2002, signed off by the White House, that the Americans were going to arm the Kurds by the summer of 2002.

However, the White House had sent nothing to the Kurds.

The Kurds told Sam in late August 2002, "Look, there is a huge Iraqi force on the ground in the North. There is going to be a lag between the time Saddam knows you are coming for him, and the time you actually have significant forces on the ground in Iraq. Saddam will have plenty of time to launch chemical and biological missiles at our Kurdish cities and towns."

So, in late August 2002, in Erbil and up on the Green Line, General Amin was very justified in pressing Sam and the counterterrorists, asking them time and again, "When are you going to arm us? When are the planes coming? When are the tanks coming?" That issue, of when the supplies were going to come for the Kurds, just became bigger and bigger the longer the counterterrorists were behind enemy lines in Iraq.

Folks who assumed that the Kurds would always stay in the fight with the Americans, shoulder to shoulder, come hell or high water, were really missing a crucial element of the counterterrorists' covert operation in Iraq.

The Kurds would have been completely justified had they looked Sam and the counterterrorists in the eye and said, "The White House hasn't honored any of their commitments. War is not imminent; Bush has no plan of attack. U.S. Army 10th Group Special Forces is not coming, and neither is U.S. Army 4th Infantry Division."

The White House made a command decision, finally, in late August, telling Sam and the counterterrorists, "Return stateside and pull together more teams; you'll return to Kurdistan as soon as you've regrouped."

NO JOY ON
THIS FREQUENCY
Kurdistan, October–December 2002

On October 2, 2002, Sam and his team readied to cross the Harburr River once again. As they waited there in broad daylight on the Turkish border, with their fleet of jeeps and trucks, they discovered something: The White House had been hustled by one of Saddam Hussein's former officers, known simply as "The General," who had convinced the White House of his valor inside the Beltway.

Unlike the Kurdish leadership, The General had never led any guerrillas in battle against Saddam's Iraqi Army, nor had he carried out any clandestine operations against Saddam's *Mukhabarat*.

Nevertheless, the White House was impressed by The General, and had put a strong arm on Tenet, directing that The General's Sunni Arab raiding force enjoy the largesse of the American defense and intelligence budget. The General would be leading this group of supremely motivated warriors in fighting trim. Their name: the Scorpions.

According to Tenet in his memoirs, the Scorpions were a heroic force, and would be vital to ending Saddam Hussein's regime. Sam, however, had quite a different understanding of the group:

The General well and truly laid the con down on Washington, straight-up hustle for the almighty dollar. He proposed a huge, multimillion-dollar project to train and equip an Iraqi Arab force, which would then be deployed back in-country to conduct sabotage and other guerrilla operations.

The whole thing crashed and burned. It was a nightmare from the beginning, with massive problems.

Basically everything that Tenet says about the Scorpions in his book is a crock of shit.

I don't know if Tenet really knows how out of touch he is on that point in his memoirs, or if he is just deliberately lying to cover his ass. He makes it sound like a great success, when in fact it was an unmitigated disaster.

We at the Salahuddin base ultimately conducted a tremendous amount of covert action (sabotage ops and paramilitary operations), and it was all conducted as a result of programs which we generated in-country, with very limited resources and with the cooperation of the KDP. Ninety-nine percent of our manpower was Kurdish *peshmerga,* from the KDP.

The Scorpion effort was something completely different from that. It was supposed to be a force composed exclusively of Iraqi Arabs, not Kurds.

The Scorpions were supposed to be able to conduct a whole gamut of paramilitary operations— sabotage, raids, platoon/company strength, operating out of vehicles and choppers—a very ambitious program that achieved nothing. They were supposed to operate out of Kurdistan, and also neighboring countries of Iraq.

When the American counterterrorists went in the second time, in October 2002, they had full teams for Salahuddin and Qal'ah Chulan; they very shortly discovered, at the border, just how the White House plans for the Scorpions jeopardized their own security. The original plan was to go to Salahuddin and set up the base; then the counterterrorist team leader for Qal'ah Chulan would move on, with his team, to the far ridgelines of the Zagros Mountains in Qal'ah Chulan, deep in southern Kurdistan.

"Obviously, we had a lot of security concerns," Sam said in a bar in Washington on Thanksgiving weekend, 2007, with Cassandra Wilson singing her poignant cover of a Hank Williams classic, "I'm So Lonesome I Could Cry," from speakers built into the brick walls of the saloon.

It was a big convoy, very visible, with a lot of people in the loop. We were very conscious that our enemies—Saddam's *Mukhabarat,* Al-Qaeda, and Ansar al-Islam—had a lot of sources throughout Northern Iraq. We knew Saddam's secret police desperately wanted to kill us.

We didn't have forty people who'd trained together for this kind of operation. We had forty people thrown together, drop of a hat, for the covert movement.

Headquarters called us on the Turkish border, on the cusp, day before the movement. They started talking to me about the Scorpions program, which I was aware of. The General was recruiting, supposedly, inside Iraq. I knew that this was on the agenda, and once set up at our two bases, we'd have to start working on getting the Scorpions some recruits.

Iraq Operations Group at CIA headquarters told me, "Hey, The General says he has a hundred guys, and they are all top-notch, all ready to go, operational, highly motivated, ready to attack Saddam, and he has assembled them all. We're going to tell him to have those guys cross over into Turkey, right now, and we want you, right now, to split your team. We want you to meet them and process them in Turkey, get them on aircraft, and they will fly to the U.S. and we will train them here."

"First of all," I replied, from my position on the border, "are the Turks on board with this? You're telling me that one hundred Iraqi Arab strangers, that I don't have a clue about, are now going to magically be allowed into Turkey? Then, we are going to materialize, from somewhere, a place to house and feed them. I reckon we're going to produce an aircraft from somewhere, because they are not going to fly commercial to the United States."

Neither Tenet, nor anyone in the White House or the Agency, had thought this through at all.

We had a massive logjam with the Turks on air transit and air rights that had already compromised us significantly.

Headquarters' response was, predictably, "No, we don't have any of that moving. None of that is on the ground. We're just going to call Ankara and get this sorted out. We should be able to have one of our aircraft in Turkey, by tomorrow."

On the border, I told headquarters, "Here's the situation: No. I will not do this.

"No joy on this frequency regarding the Scorpions.

"I have no reason on earth to believe that you can get the Turks, overnight, to agree to something like this. And you're asking me to drop everything and do this, just as I'm getting ready to cross into Iraq and execute a very dangerous maneuver, one of the most dangerous I can carry out with a platoon-sized covert unit. We are going to be exposed, in daylight, on roads, during the entire movement."

Part of that movement was going into Dahuk, and we had to pass through the artillery fan of the Iraqi Army, right across the Green Line: all the big guns of Iraqi Army 5th Corps, all of Saddam's 105mm cannons, 120s, and 155s at Dormeez.

And, of course, Saddam had all kinds of *Mukhabarat* based out of Dormeez, a real rat's nest for Baathist spies, a dagger pointed at Dahuk and all of northern Kurdistan.

Clandestine-wise, Dormeez was the last place you'd ever want to deal with, but we had to pass it in broad daylight. A real chokepoint.

Now, not only was headquarters asking me to split the team, but it was worse than that. If I was going to send my guys to deal with The General's supposed paramilitary force, and process them and get them into Turkey, that means I would have to take all my best snipers, for example, and remove them from the convoy, that instant.

I would have been taking the guys that I was really counting on to protect us and protect our convoy, and handing them over to deal with the Scorpions, just when I most needed my guys to secure the convoy as we were preparing to go in harm's way.

I also pointed out to headquarters: "All you know is that The General inside the Beltway claims he has a hundred guys in Iraq, and nobody has laid eyes on these guys. You're now going to try to bring them out of Iraq and into Turkey?"

That meant we would have been taking responsibility for them. With both the Turks and the Kurds, we would have been telling them, "We're responsible for this mysterious Iraqi Arab raiding force."

So, what happens if we get them into Turkey, start processing them, and discover that for any one of a thousand reasons, they are not acceptable—they've got dysentery or syphilis, or they're criminals, or they're seventy years old, and The General is just padding his numbers, because Washington was paying The General by the guy—so what are we going to do with them?

And the answer is, "We're going to send them back to Iraq," so I told headquarters, "Well, what if they won't go back to Iraq? How are we supposed to make them go back if they should decide not to?"

Roger that; headquarters hadn't thought of that, at all. Nearly all of these guys were from Western Iraq, Baghdad, and Central Iraq.

The Scorpions were not native to Northern Iraq or Kurdistan—and the Kurds didn't like them anyway.

Assuming that the Kurds allowed them to transit, and we got them into Turkey, and one of them turns out to be a friggin' thief or a murderer or rapist, and we have to send him back into Iraq, the Kurds are no doubt going to say, "Wait a minute—the only reason we allowed him to transit through Kurdistan is because the CIA, you mob of white boys with Southern accents and blue jeans and sidearms, told us that he'd be going into Turkey. And now a known rapist is coming back into Kurdistan?"

So, I told headquarters, "This is what I am going to do. I am going, in an orderly fashion, into Salahuddin.

"I'm going to set up my base there, get communications up, make sure security is squared away.

"We will separate all gear for Qal'ah Chulan. Then, we will get in contact with The General's people, and we will start processing his guys—looking at counterintelligence issues, medical issues, personal history, criminal background—and we'll make a cut.

"The guys that meet our standards, that look like they have a chance of actually doing something effective for us, we will send them into Turkey at that point. And that gives you guys time to make all the arrangements that you haven't made yet, for onward movement of the Scorpions out of Turkey."

Headquarters said, "Okay." Headquarters was unhappy, but they weren't going to order me to split my team. We set up in Salahuddin.

Within the first week that we were there, we made contact with The General's people. We arranged for him to bring the Scorpions to a hotel, in the vicinity of Shaqlawa.

We arranged for him to bring his guys there, and meanwhile, we basically took over the hotel. I had to talk to the KDP to arrange all this. So, I was talking with Masrour Barzani and explaining all this.

Masrour's response was, "Absolutely, we want to help you guys." But he went on to say, "Look, if you need skilled commandos to carry out sabotage and covert operations, raids, *I've got thousands of them.*

"They are called *peshmerga.* They long ago proved their fighting spirit and willingness to take down Saddam. If you want to give them more training, fine, but why don't you use them, instead of trying to create from scratch, out of very questionable material, this new force?"

Meanwhile, Massoud and Masrour were explicitly, especially Masrour in this conversation, asking, "Where are those anti-tank weapons and all the other weapons and supplies you guys promised us months ago?"

I was in close contact with Masrour, and he'd often say, throughout this time, "I'm a little confused here, Sam. You, the CIA, promised us a bunch of stuff in February, which by the way I haven't seen any of, and now you want me to help you arm and train an Arab force—for missions that we both know they, maybe, slim maybe, will actually be able to carry out. And which my guys are already very capable of conducting, right now, and I have a helluva lot more than one hundred."

My response to Masrour was, "We want to train this force because we feel it's important to have an Arab force here. We will get you what we promised and we will stand by you." It was a difficult conversation to have with Masrour because my team, all of us, agreed with Masrour.

And we were saying precisely the same thing to our own headquarters that Masrour had said to us: "Where are the promised weapons for the Kurds? And why the hell are we trying to train an Arab force from scratch, when there are tens of thousands of trained, experienced, and committed forces—Kurdish *peshmerga*—who will throw down on Saddam, right now?"

'The other dynamic at play here, with guys like The General and Ahmed Chalabi, is that they knew how to work Washington. They knew which palm to grease inside the Beltway, and also, how to play "cover your ass." [Author's Note: Ahmed Chalabi was an Iraqi exile who'd lived in London and the United States since 1958. Chalabi hustled Washington in 2002 on his Arab Resistance Fighter Army, heir to the courage of the French Resistance in World War II, when in fact Chalabi did not have one Iraqi Arab loyal to him taking arms against Saddam.

Chalabi was a liar and not to be trusted, plain and simple.]

So, we sent a team to Shaqlawa, north of Sala-huddin, to survey the Scorpions, and Doc was on the team. He had been on Johnny "Mike" Spann's team in Afghanistan. We sent a relatively small team, maybe half a dozen guys. Doc is a great guy; he's not only a medic, but also as good a ground branch officer as anybody, squared away. Doc was really concerned about this whole thing. It had only been a year since Spann had died at Mazar-e-Sharif.

My guys were walking into a meeting with one hundred strangers and nobody had any idea of who these guys really were. We could have been sur-rounded and killed, just like Spann was. And this was in an area where Saddam's *Mukhabarat* was all over the place.

Doc said, "If we're going to do this, then I don't care what headquarters thinks, we will treat these guys as hostiles until they prove otherwise."

I told him, "That's great, absolutely. Do it. Our personal security comes first."

That's how our guys rolled in, everyone gunned up, ready to rock and roll. Our guys herded the hundred or so Scorpions outside the hotel, bring-ing them in, one at a time. They patted them down and screened them, with ground branch officers and case officers and U.S. Army Special Forces locked and loaded at all times. The senior alleged Scorpion guy was just incensed that we treated his guys like this, but Johnny "Mike" Spann was on our minds, at all times. [Author's Note: Johnny "Mike" Spann, a native of Alabama, graduate of Auburn University and former U.S. Marine Captain, was a CIA clandestine field officer killed by Al-Qaeda and Taliban prisoners in a riot at a prison near Mazar-e-Sharif, Afghanistan, on November 25, 2001. The Al-Qaeda terrorist John Walker Lindh, a Californian, was one of the prisoners who plotted and carried out the riot. The CIA honored Spann, as with all officers killed on active service, with a star on a memorial wall at CIA headquarters in Langley, Virginia. Spann is the 79th star.]

Many of us knew Mike Spann as a friend and comrade. We weren't going to let what happened to Mike happen to us. So, our guys told the Scorpions' gadfly in-country, "You can follow the instructions. And if you can't do that, you can just walk away."

It was just a nightmare with the Scorpions. They were losers.

There were all sorts of medical problems, of epic proportions. There were guys with criminal backgrounds.

None of them had ever thrown down against Saddam.

Most of them, as I recall, had no commitment to taking down Saddam. It was strictly a money jungle for the Scorpions; they, like The General, were just there to navigate Washington's money jungle.

The General's guys had just scooped up most of them from the desert and villages throughout Iraq—just a bunch of bums.

Remember, The General got paid for every head.

Headquarters, meanwhile, kept telling us, "The Scorpions are fully committed to taking down Saddam. They are all followers of The General. They are just chomping at the bit to bring freedom to Iraq."

Baseline, even the ones who didn't have medical or criminal records—about all you could say is that they were just looking for a paycheck. So we went ahead and processed these guys. Out of that first group, we moved maybe twenty-five guys into Turkey. And they did go. We took them to the border, a few weeks later.

The whole Scorpions boondoggle compromised us operationally when it came to counterterrorist missions, thirteen months after September 11th. It also hurt us with clandestine missions. The Scorpions were just a colossal fucking waste of time.

Headquarters did train these guys thoroughly—weapons, demolition, and tradecraft. Some of them were supposed to be used in small teams, and some in larger raids. CIA bought all kinds of gear. The Scorpions had their own air force, attack and transport choppers—a real high-speed raiding force, on paper.

When the conventional war started, they were supposed to conduct raids. They did not conduct raids. The Scorpions were a disaster.

Ultimately, headquarters detailed Snake, a ground branch officer, to deal with the Scorpions. Snake is the same guy who saved Karzai's life in Afghanistan in December 2001. He is a former Reconnaissance Marine, and brilliant—one of the best minds in the Agency and one of the most respected ground branch officers we have.

He went into a country bordering Iraq. Headquarters sent him there to get them stood up and make them start doing something, after January 2003.

Snake declared the Scorpions unfit for combat. He told headquarters, "The Scorpions cannot perform any of the missions you have trained them for. I am not putting any of my guys on any raid with them, in the first place, or any other mission. We are going to get good men killed for no reason. These guys are worthless."

Now, the Scorpions were supposed to deploy small sabotage teams to infiltrate across the Green Line and blow up specific targets, like rail lines. Only one such team was ever sent back to us inside Northern Iraq. We parked these four guys in a safe house and they sat for months, waiting for the war to start.

We spent a lot of time keeping these guys under the radar, while making sure they were fed and entertained, and receiving constant refresher training sessions.

The art of blowing up rail lines is far more difficult than it seems. If you don't do it exactly right in terms of the placement and size of the charges, you just scatter the rails all over the place. And it doesn't take much time for a repair crew to put down new ties and lay down new rail. You have to know exactly what you are doing; it's kind of an art to cut the rails properly and really disrupt rail traffic.

That one Scorpions team in the safe house—their primary mission was to take out rail lines. They'd been given all kinds of specialized training.

When the air war started and we were initiating sabotage ops, those four remaining Scorpions got the green light to go into Iraqi territory and hit a rail line outside Mosul. The Scorpions mutinied in early March 2003, saying, "We are afraid and we want to go home now." I sent them to a neighboring country.

The Kurds were just completely beside themselves. They had constantly told us, over and over again, "Why are you wasting your time with these idiots?"

The Kurds and my team were right from the beginning, and Washington was just so wrong.

Roger that; Washington historically does not listen to field intelligence, and, yet again, Washington failed to listen to those of us in the field.

The Scorpions never carried out a mission in Iraq, despite the fact that Tenet describes them as a heroic force. They were neither a force, nor in any way heroic. They were losers.

When I finally left Iraq, on a U.S. Air Force C-17, we flew from Hareer, which was held by the 173rd

Airborne at that time, north of Erbil, of course. We flew into a neighboring Arab country and sat on the tarmac, waiting. There was a hangar at this airfield where the Scorpion air force was based. Some of our guys assigned there talked to us, and we got up and walked through the hangar, which was just filled with HIND helicopters, Mi-17s, millions of dollars' worth of air assets, all painted with scorpions logos, and they all looked bright and shiny and brand-new.

My Dahuk counterterrorist team leader looked at me and said, "We liberated Northern Iraq on a shoestring, with everything we cobbled together, and look at what they gave these assholes. Can you imagine what we could have done with even one chopper? Headquarters gave these guys millions and millions of dollars, and they never did a damn thing with them."

Tenet's heroic force had all kinds of problems. Among other things, the Scorpions were raping each other during training which poses its own set of problems: What do you do when people start committing felonies in training, on a black site,? They're committing felonies, but officially, they don't exist, and the place we're training them is not acknowledged. They were not motivated to take down Saddam, but they volunteered all the time to rape each other up the ass. You can imagine how many different places this was happening.

The whole Scorpion issue made no sense to the Kurds, and it made no sense to us, either. We told headquarters from jump street on the Scorpions, "This is just a fuckin' waste of time, money, and effort. It makes no sense. These guys are never going to accomplish a goddamn thing." That is exactly what we told headquarters, and it was relayed to the White House. But Washington had this whole World War II guerrilla resistance fantasy: "These brave Iraqi Arabs are the French Resistance of our time; they are Iraqi Arab Jedburgh teams."

We kept telling headquarters, "Bullshit! The Scorpions are from the ash heaps of Iraq, these are derelicts and bums and common criminals." If Washington had listened to us from the get-go, they would have saved a lot of money and we would have armed and trained Kurdish clandestine teams, which we ended up doing anyway but on a shoestring.

In Salahuddin, Sam and his counterterrorists and clandestine officers and U.S. Army Special Forces commandos reunited with the Kurdish leadership, unloaded all their gear, and set up their base.

In early October 2002, they had a little over twenty people inside the base. Everybody was pumped to be there, to be back in-country.

Sam and his men, and two women clandestine officers, had shared the feeling of, "We're finally here. We can get to work."

On the other hand, when Sam sat down in Salahuddin, and his Qal'ah Chulan team leader gathered a smaller counterterrorist team at their fire base in southern Kurdistan, they faced very daunting clandestine missions, making an already-complex operation even more complicated.

They had a whole stack of different missions to do: the military prep of the battlefield for the invasion of Iraq, which entailed surveying every road, bridge, and facility in Kurdistan, with the full cooperation of the Kurds.

The Americans had to inspect every Kurdish unit and eyeball all their ammunition, supplies, and vehicles. Special Forces commandos took care of that, meeting every *peshmerga* commander in all Kurdistan throughout the fall of 2002, and well into the long, snowy winter in the Kurdish highlands.

Turkey, however, was threatening to invade Kurdistan. Sam's team now had to "keep the Turks from invading Kurdistan," Sam said in Boston in early November 2007. After lunch that day, we ordered coffee and Sam continued his account of the constant Turkish threat to invade Kurdistan and his own previous counterterrorist missions in Southeast Asia:

The Turks were threatening to invade Kurdistan in the fall of 2002, just as they are threatening to invade again now in fall 2007.

In the 1990s, I served overseas in Southeastern Europe where I was hunting Islamist terrorists. Diyarbakir was the Wild West in those days. Everywhere you walked everyone around you was armed. Jeeps, trucks, and armored cars rolled on the streets. It was an occupied city.

The other thing we were doing was cross-border intelligence operations into Iraq, basically running Iraqi assets; some of those were Arabs, some of those were Kurds. During this time there were NILE [Northern Iraq Liaison Element] teams intermittently placed throughout Northern Iraq.

The consensus from our Iraqi Arab and Kurdish sources was, "This is great. I'm happy to tell you all this, but what I really want to know is, when are you getting rid of Saddam? You should have taken him down in 1991; when are you getting rid of him?"

We were in a constant holding pattern throughout 1995 and 1996, running assets and collecting information, and sort of asking everybody to be patient.

It's important, however, to understand that our Kurdish and Arab assets were not looking at this like an academic exercise.

This was very real for them; they were risking their lives and their families' lives just by talking to us.

Keep in mind that during this time period, our assets in Iraq were dying all the time, in absolutely horrific fashion. It's not pretty when Saddam's *Mukhabarat* captures you, tortures you, and kills you.

There was a situation when Saddam's *Mukhabarat* captured one of our Arab sources with communications gear, called us up, and laughed into the phone as they tortured our guy to death. You could hear him being tortured to death.

People were dying for us, but we were still in hover mode. Fact of the matter is, we had no real answers for them, because Washington couldn't make up its mind. Clinton didn't know what to do. I stayed in counterterrorism ops against Islamist terrorists. The Turks lost a lot of soldiers, fighting against the PKK. A lot of mothers weeping in Istanbul and Ankara and Izmir, and all of Turkey, for their sons who did not come back from southeastern Turkey.

I remember sitting on an airfield in Diyarbakir, in the middle of one of those ops, and we had just come off an operation.

There was a steady string of Huey medevac flights, a long line of red lights flashing, choppers coming in with a lot of dead and wounded. Very vicious fighting. The kind of fighting where if you're wounded and captured, you don't survive. Mutilated bodies.

You look at that kind of hatred that exists on both sides, and both sides can find reasons to hate each other even more.

The Turks, clearly, have been fighting a long counterterrorist and guerrilla war against the PKK, for decades, and it's often really brutal and vicious. But it will not end until Kurds in Turkey see and feel and know that they are respected the same as Turks, that there is dignity in Kurdish lives and communities in Turkey, and that the Kurds in Turkey feel like they have an equal voice, an equal future, in Turkey.

I remember being in Diyarbakir at *Nawrouz,* Kurdish New Year, in March 1997. There were fires everywhere, with Kurds marching and celebrating in the *Nawrouz* parades, holding candles and torches.

The Kurds would light rubber tires everywhere as a deliberate protest. The Turks didn't react, even though you had hundreds of thousands of people lighting these fires. The sky was just black with smoke. It was the Kurdish way of saying, "You may be sitting on us, and you may control the corners and the streets with armored cars and guns, but we are still here, our dignity and our honor are intact, and we are still defiant. We will resist until we see real justice and real dignity for our people, for our children and for our future."

When you'd fly in a chopper over southeastern Turkey, you'd fly over one Kurdish village after another where nobody lived anymore.

All the roofs were gone from the stone houses and all the buildings were destroyed.

And the internal Kurdish refugees, from uprooted villages in Turkey, were just shoved into slums in Diyarbakir.

I remember the Turks used to create landing pads for their choppers by leveling the tops of small hills and hillocks, all over southeastern Turkey. Just places for Cobras to sit. You'd just see them sitting there, positioned all over the place, because that's how frequently the Turks had to call in those Cobras for air support.

If you're really talking about ending the Kurdish insurgency in Turkey, however, if you want to end the PKK as a terrorist organization, then you have to deal with and resolve the fundamental root causes.

At that time, in the 1990s, Kurdish language radio was forbidden in Turkey, so Kurds couldn't listen to their music in their own language.

Kurdish newspapers were also forbidden. We used to say to the Turks, all the time, "If I'm an eighteen-year-old Kurdish kid in Diyarbakir, I've got no money, no job, and everywhere I look, there are Turkish soldiers who are not Kurds and don't speak Kurdish and don't respect me, my culture, my history, and my language. Meanwhile, I can't afford to get married because I have committed the crime in Turkey of having been born a Kurd."

Now, a Kurdish man comes down out of a mountain in southeastern Turkey, where Kurds have lived for six thousand years, and says to me, in Kurdish, "Come with me, brother, and you can be a man and liberate our people from the Turkish yoke."

Chances are pretty good that I am going to take him up on his offer, because the Turks are not offering any other options.

By the same token, if I'm Kurdish and eighteen in Diyarbakir and I've got a job and I'm putting money in the bank in southeastern Turkey, so I can tell the gal that I've got eyes for, "Let's meet the preacher man," and now she's got my engagement ring on her finger, then I am in no big hurry to live in a cave with a bunch of guys with guns and stale bread and plastic explosives.

If the Turks want the Kurds to buy into the system, then they have to let them enjoy the benefits of the system.

Just over a year after September 11th, in 2002, my counterterrorist officers and case officers in Kurdistan—still working with Kurds night and day, and fully committed to taking down Al-Qaeda in the Near East—were also still hunting Ansar al-Islam. Total Kurdish support on that front, too. Ansar al-Islam had a whole bunch of cells in Erbil, and they were growing like an octopus in fall 2002.

We had our work cut out for us, as we were also going after Saddam, across the Green Line, of course. So, we bore down on the situation with the Kurds, which involved convincing Iraqis to cross the Green Line to meet with us, at great risk to themselves, obviously, and it involved sending Kurds out beyond the Green Line, again at great risk.

It became a very hard business. We grabbed ahold of every thread we could and pulled. Initially, some of the case officers were having a very hard time with the level of physical risk that we were exposing our assets to. Very early on, we saw a fair number of individuals defecting from Saddam's regime, and saying, "I'll talk to you, but I need you to protect me and my family, and house us."

We were flat on our ass, and needed sources inside Saddam's Iraq. And here's Abdul, who's crossed the Green Line, saying, "I quit, I'm out; can you get me to America, or at the very least, get me a house here, because I'm not going back." Our attitude was basically, "We're going to make maximum effort with these guys not just to debrief them, but also to turn them back inside Iraq."

So, we told the first sources, "It's not that easy; we need you back inside."

Some of our sources were just rats off a sinking ship. You know: "I've been torturing people to death for ten years, but Saddam's going down, and now I'm on your side."

Obviously, the potential danger of forcing them to go back inside was extreme. Even some of our case officers, who early on were having trouble with all of this, recognized the potential for them to get killed. They were having a really hard time pressuring them to go back inside Iraq.

In late October 2002, we had a meeting at Salahuddin with all twenty of our case officers, a reality check on our sources inside Saddam's regime: "Look, it's not a matter of getting ready to go to war. As far as we're concerned, we're already at war, and Saddam's regime is our enemy. You're a murdering sonuvabitch, but you're our source, and where we need you is in Mosul or Baghdad, reporting for us. And if you don't go back, I'll turn you over to the Kurds. You're a war criminal. And they'll deal with you."

I remember there was one guy on my team who got very emotional about a specific case, right then. And I told him, "If you can't tell your source exactly that, I will. We have to make some hard choices."

He replied to me, "If I send these guys back, I have no guarantee that they are not going to be killed. They left, and their absence may already be noted."

Typically, what a source from Baghdad would do is take leave and say, "I'm going to visit Grandma in Mosul."

Then, he'd smuggle himself across the Green Line. Now, say it's three days into his ten-day or two-week leave. Maybe he can go back to his office in Baghdad.

It's also possible that somebody has already checked up on him and learned that he's not at Grandma's house. Or he's cleaned out his bank account and betrayed to some security service that he's not coming back to Baghdad.

So, maybe he can go back and pretend he was in Mosul, and maybe he'll be cool. Or maybe he'll show up at his desk and some goons will appear and whisk him away to some god-awful torture that will kill him. It's a crapshoot.

This particular case ended up being the center point of the meeting in Salahuddin in late October 2002. This case officer was saying, "We're going to get them killed."

My response was, "Look, I don't care. We are at war here already, and war means sending some people to their deaths in order to save far more people. One thing I can guarantee that is going to happen before this war is over is that a lot of Americans are going to get killed here. And if we make these guys go back, the information they can provide us is going to save hundreds of thousands of lives."

Remember that in the fall of 2002, there were already estimates of at least 25,000 U.S. combat deaths in the first year of the Iraq War. And that was coming right from the Pentagon. The American and international media estimated even higher numbers of Americans and our allies killed in action. And, of course, we were working against the backdrop of weapons of mass destruction.

Bottom line to my case officer in Salahuddin: "You're right. It's entirely possible that our sources in Saddam's regime may get killed. And if it's them versus American lives, they don't equate. I'm not eager to get our assets killed, but that's unavoidable—that's the cost of doing business here. We are here to save American lives and win the war."

He was shocked—and more than a little pissed off. His reaction, and the reaction of some of the guys on the team . . . they were just shocked. In their view, I was extremely callous in being willing to do this. And I told them, "If you won't deliver the message, I will."

In this specific case, the sources involved had made their careers in Saddam's regime, torturing people and executing people. These were *Mukhabarat* and Iraqi security services, and now these bastards were in Kurdistan, and they definitely didn't want to talk to the Kurds.

But they did want to talk to us, absolve themselves of their sins, and get paid for their information. My conviction with all of them was that if this murdering sonuvabitch dies because he gave us juice on Saddam, I'm not gonna lose any sleep at night—especially if it saves American lives and helps win the war.

To his credit, this particular case officer did deliver the message, and his sources did go back to Baghdad and provide a lot of valuable information. They were ultimately discovered and killed by *Mukhabarat.*

I remember talking with the same case officer, after the *Mukhabarat* had killed his sources, and he asked me, "*Now* do you regret your decision? I told you we were going to get these guys killed, and now they are dead."

"I'm not happy we got them killed," I told him, "but it has no impact whatsoever on my decision, and we are going to continue doing precisely the same thing. This is a war and people are going to die. If you can't handle the fact that we are in a war and people are going to die—and you are going to send some of them to their deaths—then we're going to have to put you in a vehicle and send you home."

We ended up with a little over twenty folks on the ground in Salahuddin, fall of 2002, and not all Agency. We had three commandos from 10th Group Special Forces, and folks from Special Operations, also.

A key dynamic from October to December was that a bit of tribalism seeped in.

You had the case officers looking at the ground branch guys with the attitude, "You're knuckle-draggers; you're not real Intel guys."

The ground branch guys were looking at the case officers, thinking, "If anything goes wrong, you just get behind me and pray I stay alive because I am the only thing that is going to save your ass."

Then, you've got all the Agency guys looking at the Special Forces guys, like, "You're just a bunch of grunts; we don't know *why* you are here."

And the Special Forces guys are saying, "We just can't believe that this is how you guys do business; you're just kind of making up everything as you go along. There is no TOE [Table of Organization and Equipment, standard structure for any military unit], and there is no goddamn field manual on anything you do."

Well, I sat the case officers down and told them, "I don't want to hear any more shit about any differentiation here. I don't want to hear any more bullshit about this being an Agency team, why is U.S. military here, why are Special Ops here, and anything related.

"We are all Americans here, and we are all on this mission, together.

"One mission, one team.

"And this bullshit about the case officers being here, and 'We don't need ground branch.' First of all, this is an American team and we are an American mission. We are here to win the war and get home alive.

"And second, before we're done with this whole thing, we're going to need all the skills and abilities of *everyone* here, from all their different backgrounds. Stop playing this *them and us* game."

In one case, I had to pull in a case officer—I'll call him Dick—who continued to make disrespectful comments.

Dick kept making disparaging remarks, just looking to fuck with our Special Forces honchos. The immediate issue was that Dick was making significantly more money than them, and for some reason, Dick thought it was real cool to keep reminding these guys of how much money he was putting away, for doing the same exact work.

The immediate problem, of course, was that if he didn't shut his mouth, Special Forces were gonna kill him—in his sleep, no doubt. Obviously, this whole thing was destructive and a real distraction. We were simultaneously trying to create the team and build cohesion while we were already moving a thousand miles an hour.

Well, I set up a special meeting, just for Dick. I told him, "Dick, you are going to respect everyone here and figure out that we are one team, or you are going home. End of transmission."

After that sit-down, Dick kept his mouth shut.

We did all of this without a template. It's hard enough to forge together a rifle company or a platoon. For that, even, you've got a fairly defined structure: TOE, method of operation, field manuals, and so on. We had to create this entire clandestine team, with folks from many different branches and backgrounds, and nobody involved had any experience with such a team.

There was no precedent for this. Nobody had done this before, on clandestine operations. We had to invent it while we were already at war.

But we came together. One mission, one team.

Mighty cold in December in the Kurdish highlands, but the Kurds gave us kerosene heaters, and we had heavy-duty mountain sleeping bags. We kept it light, playing "Lowrider" at all hours, grooving, cutting up. Gray, cold winter, deep in the Zagros Mountains, plenty of snow and ice. And choice smuggled coffee, thank God, and the Kurds.

CLANDESTINE MEETINGS WITH THE SHIA AND THE KURDS, AND HUNTING SADDAM'S SECRET POLICE

Kurdistan, January–March 2003

In early January of 2003, the Kurds revealed to Sam and his team at Salahuddin that they had long-standing contacts with senior Shia political leaders from the south. Sam shared this historic information with the counterterrorists, and sent the intelligence directly to CIA headquarters, which relayed it to the White House.

The Kurds were already well down the road with the Shia in talking about what post-Saddam Iraq was going to look like.

The Kurds had been careful not to tell the White House this, and the Bush administration was largely ignorant of the Shia-Kurdish relationship.

No one, for instance, in the CIA nor the White House had ordered Sam's team to gather intelligence on contacts and relationships between Shia tribal chieftains in Southern Iraq and Kurdish political leaders in Kurdistan, in light of the fact that the Shia and the Kurds comprise 80 percent of Iraq's population—and both the Kurds and the Shia had suffered horribly under the Baathist dictatorship of Saddam Hussein.

The Kurds are pretty good at playing their cards close to the vest and keeping their own counsel when dealing with the United States—not surprising, of course, given how American governments have betrayed them in the past.

"The White House, and the senior levels of the CIA, did not want to believe that the Kurds had these kinds of contacts," Sam said in a bar in Philadelphia in early December 2007. We were drinking Kentucky bourbon and listening to Stan Getz play "My Foolish Heart" from a stereo system that disappeared somewhere below the bar, the speakers concealed in the ceiling throughout the ornate brass and wood and brick-built saloon.

Sam went on, talking at length about how the White House believed the lies of Ahmed Chalabi, an Iraqi exile who'd lived in London and the United States since 1958.

Washington continued to fail to listen to the field intelligence coming from the American counterterrorists and clandestine field officers in Kurdistan and Northern Iraq throughout the winter of 2003, Sam noted. He stated that throughout the gray, cold winter in the icy, snowy, and muddy highlands of Kurdistan, "The Kurds were our only friends." Sam continued:

Without the Kurds, we would've been starved out, as the Turks barred our supplies, including food, from crossing the border.

Fortunately, the Kurds reached out to us through contacts they'd made with the Shia. We had some initial discussions with Masrour Barzani, head of

KDP intelligence, in early January 2003, in regard to Shia-Kurdish relations. He told us that a number of senior Shia folks had been in contact with him. So, he proposed a meeting.

We told Washington, but both the White House and our headquarters refused to believe us.

"We do not believe the Kurds are talking with the Shia," they said. It's kind of strange when you consider that an intelligence community exists to discover something others don't know, and to bring it to their attention. Ultimately, it is my duty, and of course, my job, to get previously undiscovered information to the highest levels of American command, to save American lives.

However, when you actually discover something that the highest levels of command, including the President, don't know, they tell you it can't be true because they didn't already know it. This was especially true with the administration of the forty-third presidency.

"We don't have any information to corroborate this," the White House would relay to us, which is code for, "We didn't already know this, so it can't be true." When you get into these situations, you think, "So what is the point of even having an intelligence service, since no one is listening to the field intelligence we are collecting and analyzing?"

We got a lot of pushback, and headquarters was saying, "We're not saying the Kurds have *no* contacts with the Shia, but they must be exaggerating their contacts."

The other thing we got from headquarters: "There is no way in hell that Shia leaders from Southern Iraq could transit to Kurdish areas."

From 10,000 miles away, headquarters made amazing judgments about what can and cannot be done in Iraq.

We'd seen stuff move across the Green Line all the time. We were constantly running assets across the Green Line. In addition to our wits, we relied on cash. And like all of our additional vehicles, we'd procured Land Cruisers, in-country. We'd smuggled half of the vehicles we were driving through the entirety of Iraq, from Basra to Mosul.

Now, headquarters was telling me that Shia Iraqis, born and raised in the Near East, with a lifetime of contacts and connections inside Iraq and across Europe, Asia, and the Near East, fluent in Arabic and Iraqi dialects, could not do what we'd done.

With much skepticism, headquarters gave us guidance on dealing with Shia-Kurdish political relationships, finally saying, "Okay, if you want to waste your time, go ahead, but we have the great crystal ball on our desks here at Langley, and we know you will fail."

Well, we went ahead, without a crystal ball.

One guy we met in Salahuddin, a Shia chieftain, claimed to speak on behalf of a very broad coalition of political leaders from the South, all Shia. In this initial meeting, he was trying to find out if we were serious.

The shadow of 1991 was hanging over this whole discussion. We spent a lot of time listening to him talk about 1991. Basically he said, "What the fuck? It sounded pretty clear to us that you'd support our revolt, and Bush's father called for us to revolt against Saddam in 1991. Well, we revolted and got hammered by Saddam, and you all never showed."

This was the first opportunity he'd had to talk to any Americans. We just needed to let this guy talk to us, and really unload; ten years of anger, frustration, and grief came pouring out of him. He'd lost nearly everyone in his family.

It came down to one basic thing during this meeting, as in so many meetings with the Shia: "Why the hell should I believe you Americans now? How do I know you are serious? How do I know that Bush the Younger won't just walk away, like Bush the Elder did in '91?"

Of course, we were laying out the plan for him, with 4th Infantry Division and 10th Group Special Forces, and he was looking at us and the Kurds were looking at us, all thinking, "You Americans keep talking a good game about ending Saddam's days, like you did in 1991, but talk is cheap, and all I see is a handful of guys with some sidearms and rifles."

We could see clearly that this Shia leader had a very good relationship with the Kurds, and that overall, the Kurds and the Shia had a solid, long-standing relationship.

It doesn't take a genius to figure out that in a post-Saddam environment, the Kurds and the Shia will run Iraq. These guys were already making plans to do just this, and no one in the American government had a clue about it. The CIA didn't know anything about it; no one in the White House knew anything about it; no one at the Pentagon or Foggy Bottom had a clue.

So no one stateside would believe us, since they didn't know about it before we did.

We kept trying to tell Washington, "It's wonderful that you are sitting back there in your ivory tower, making plans for what we're going to do with Iraq after we take down Saddam, but you might want to pay attention to the fact that the Shia and the Kurds already have plans of their own. They are 80 percent of this country, *and they live here."*

What we got back from Washington, at this point, was grudging acceptance that the Kurds were talking to some Shia in the south, but basically the conviction in Washington was, "This can't be of any real significance."

Roger that; it was the same dynamic playing out that is unfortunate but real in American intelligence, which is, "We have the fifty-pound brains over here, and if we don't already know about it stateside, then it doesn't exist, so don't tell us that you found it in the hills over there, where no English is spoken."

We had at least two more meetings, at which the Shia chieftain brought out sizable delegations from the south, including many Shia sheikhs.

Despite the fact that Washington said it was impossible, they came all the way up to Kurdistan. We met them in Salahuddin.

These meetings were all brokered by the Kurds, and members of the KDP were also present. We listened to a lot more rage and anger about 1991: Every Shia sheikh had a horror story about Saddam's repression of the Shia in 1991, and since.

We established a relationship with the Shia and got them to assist us. They showed us how many guys they had, and who would fight to support the invasion from the south. We were talking road junctions to secure, bridges to blow, and specific targets. Ultimately, we passed off a lot of these Shia contacts to U.S. Army 5th Group Special Forces and to our own guys, coming out of Kuwait.

The Shia forces that these sheikhs represented did, ultimately, stand and fight and participate in the invasion.

The real rub, on their side: We'd say, "We need your guys to seize such and such a village. We've distributed hundreds of satellite phones to your guys. When we give you this signal, via phone, we need you to take a bridge, or take a crossroads, to facilitate the advance from the south." Their response was, "We are with you, my brothers. As soon as I see the American tanks in my village, then we will assist you."

We'd reply, "Look, when the American tanks have taken your village, I don't need your guys in the streets." And what we didn't say, but we were thinking it, was: "The last thing I need at that point is to have your thousand guys shooting their Kalashnikovs in the air to celebrate the liberation." Instead, we said: "What I need you to do is seize the village and hold it, so the Iraqi Army doesn't blow up the bridge or mine the road."

Then, of course, they'd look very worried and say, "If we attack the Iraqis before you show up, we will be hurt badly and some of us will be shot."

When you think about the history of 1991, you can understand the Shia hesitation. Their kin died in the sands of southern Iraq because the U.S. government, during the presidency of George H. W. Bush, betrayed them. And we knew that the Shia realized how Bush had betrayed the Kurds before, and how his son, George W. Bush, had not kept any of his promises to the Kurds in 2002, either.

A real dilemma here, with the Shia chieftain and the Shia sheikhs, was that these were not guys that Washington knew, and they weren't in Washington.

They weren't Ahmed Chalabi; they weren't The General and the Scorpions; and none of them had graduated from Yale or Harvard, or owned condominiums in London or flats in Georgetown.

The Shia were not Inside the Beltway, they were Inside Iraq, and the bridges that the Kurds had built to the Shia were inside Iraq.

Since the White House hadn't paid for the concrete for those bridges, so to speak, they didn't care that the Kurds and Shia were communicating over those bridges, and what's worse, the White House didn't care that the Kurds had built the bridges to the Shia in the first place.

Now, we were talking to traditional tribal Shia sheikhs and once again, as with the Scorpions situation, what we were telling Washington was something very different from what they wanted to believe.

No one in the Bush administration ever reflected that Chalabi had not set foot in Iraq since 1958.

In contrast, the Shia sheikhs with whom we had extensive meetings in Salahuddin said, in polite Arabic, "Who the fuck is Chalabi? Why are you wasting time with him? No one knows him here. No one supports him here. He's a completely irrelevant figure."

When Chalabi arrived in-country, he came up north in February 2003.

This was his attempt to show he was a real Iraqi.

His Inside the Beltway public relations team came with him, including a female assistant. She was American, and wore a black eye patch.

We called her Pirate Chick. A very striking woman, Pirate Chick, in her twenties, and confident that Chalabi could do no wrong.

Chalabi had another American with him, also in his twenties.

We called this guy "Joe Beltway Bandit Public Relations Guy."

His real name was Francis Brooke. So, Chalabi had the Pirate Chick and the Ad Guru.

This kid was the ultimate cheesy campaign manager for some sleazy politician. No conversation with Francis Brooke had anything to do with right or wrong, or truth of any kind. Brooke was not in line when the Almighty was handing out moral compasses.

The Pentagon also sent a full-bird U.S. Army colonel with Chalabi. Now, keep in mind that we had been talking to headquarters about Chalabi for months, as the White House was in breathless mode: "Oh, this is what Chalabi says, and this is what Chalabi is going to do in Iraq once Saddam is gone, etc."

To which we'd always respond: "One more time: Nobody in Iraq knows Ahmed Chalabi, not even the dogcatchers and the gravediggers, and nobody gives a shit about him. He has no following here, he has no support, and he is irrelevant in Iraq. If Chalabi wants to run for office inside the Beltway, that's fabulous, but the Iraqis don't want anything to do with him."

But nobody paid any attention to anything we were saying. Why would they listen to us? I mean, we were the only Americans in Iraq, and it's only our sworn duty unto the death to tell you what's going down on the ground here, but what the hell would we know . . .

February 2003: Chalabi and his traveling circus were now in Iraq, and he had a compound in PUK territory, in the mountains.

Headquarters informed us that the White House wanted us to meet Chalabi at his mountain palace. Now, the 10th Group Special Forces group commander, Colonel Cleveland, was there, along with two of his battalion commanders, Lieutenant

Colonel Kenneth Tovo and Lieutenant Colonel Robert Waltemeyer.

There was also a full bird colonel, detailed as liaison to Chalabi, who was supposed to be monitoring Chalabi's activities. He was Rumsfeld's eyes on Chalabi to make sure the American government knew what Chalabi was all about.

The CIA, of course, was the only branch of the U.S. government that already had a formal position on Chalabi, which was: "Ahmed Chalabi is a liar. Do not listen to anything he says." Rumsfeld refused to believe us, however.

The first thing that struck me at the meeting was that the compound and house were the most ornate and expensive I'd seen anywhere in Kurdistan. It looked like a millionaire's country retreat on a mountain lake in Colorado. It had the feel of one of Saddam's palaces. Now I had the feeling, Ah, here is Chalabi, man of the people, who is going to lead the valiant noble uprising to take down Saddam, and he's entrenched in an extremely remote palace, not unlike Saddam's palaces.

The other thing I noted is that there were no troops.

And right away, I could see there was no Chalabi's French Resistance—no guerrilla fighters, not one rebel allied to his cause and ready to die for him. No one in Iraq was even *thinking* of fighting for him. The only people with guns at this meeting were all the security forces detailed to other people.

Chalabi ignored me for the entire meeting. He started talking, and he sounded like a snake oil salesman. *He ought to be going from town to town with a little wagon,* I thought. *Absolutely ridiculous.* He was just the biggest fool I had ever heard, and I couldn't believe anyone was taking him seriously. Chalabi was just lying his ass off, about everything.

Pirate Chick was walking around as Chalabi spoke, like she was auditioning for Johnny Depp's next skull-and-crossbones flick, and Brooke was giving me the whole nine yards: "Rah rah, Chalabi is the Future of Iraq, Chalabi is the Julius Caesar of our time, he is the Man. The New Iraq will rally around Chalabi!"

I was disgusted and walked to the back of the room. Now, Rumsfeld's eyes on Chalabi, the staff officer from the Pentagon, was also at the back of the room. I said to him, "This is such a fuckin' circus," and this U.S. Army colonel looked at me and said, "Chalabi is the future of Iraq; he is the one guy that the Iraqi people will rally around. Isn't he a great man?"

Twilight zone.

Come early March 2003, Chalabi told the White House: "I have seven hundred elite shock troops in Iraq ready to liberate the country from Saddam's regime."

That drifted around Washington, and headquarters sent us a message: "Chalabi has seven hundred elite shock troops, heavily armed, highly motivated, and they will be crucial to the invasion—real resistance fighters. Help them in every way that you can."

Our formal response, after we finished laughing, was, "We've been to Chalabi's house, and it's a very nice house, mighty comfortable, and the tea is excellent, but there are no shock troops there. There is not one Iraqi carrying a rifle in defense of Chalabi. Chalabi has many sofas and many teacups made of the finest porcelain, but Chalabi has no troops."

What Chalabi actually had were bags of money, bags of tea, and loads of bullshit.

He was not leading the resurrection of the French Resistance in our time, because he didn't have a single person carrying a weapon who was backing him.

Chalabi was a liar. He had no forces, period.

Chalabi had smoked the Department of Defense on this, and he had smoked Bush and his crew.

He had smoked Cheney, Rove, Wolfowitz, and Rice. He had smoked Rumsfeld, big time.

He had smoked the inner circle of the White House. The con man was at the top of his game, and his name was Ahmed Chalabi.

Bush refused to believe us, however. I kid you not; the official White House response was, "No, Chalabi has seven hundred shock troops, he has a base, and you simply don't know where his troops and his base are. We believe Chalabi."

Chalabi relayed to CIA headquarters, through Bush, that his shock troops were at his secret base and that we didn't know jackbone about Iraq.

Headquarters made us aware of Chalabi's protestations to the White House.

I responded to headquarters, "We've been here a very long time and our guys move all over Kurdistan and Northern Iraq. There is not a village or road that we have not been on. There is no secret base. There is no hidden, secret Chalabi fort or installation of any kind here. It doesn't exist. Chalabi is a fuckin' liar. And forget about the base: He has no shock troops. He has no troops of any kind. There is no way that he has seven hundred guys under arms in Kurdistan or anywhere else in Iraq that we, and the Kurds, do not know about."

Then, the Qal'ah Chulan base chief passed along some information that he'd received to Washington: Chalabi had made a deal with Badr Corps, a pro-Iranian Iraqi guerrilla force in opposition to Saddam. They were not friends of the United States, and it was essentially a creature of Tehran. Chalabi's plan was to use a battalion of guys who work for the Iranian regime to overthrow Saddam's regime. The Qal'ah Chulan base chief told headquarters about this in advance.

Washington said, "You are wrong, because that's not what Chalabi told us. Chalabi says that he has the seven hundred shock troops and his secret base deep in the hills, and we believe him."

This was the last thing the White House relayed to us regarding Chalabi, in early March of 2003.

The White House had simply decided that they considered Chalabi to be more trustworthy and reliable than our own CIA case officers and counter-terrorism officers on the most dangerous and sensitive clandestine operation in American history.

"The CIA must be lying to us about Chalabi, because we are the Bush White House, and Chalabi would never lie to us; he is the great, honorable Ahmed Chalabi with seven hundred valiant resistance fighters, the French Resistance of our time."

Meanwhile, as U.S. Secretary of State Colin Powell prepared to make the case at the United Nations for Saddam Hussein having weapons of mass destruction in Iraq, based on George Tenet's "slam-dunk" assessment of WMD, Sam and his team were trying to prevent the Turkish Army from invading Kurdistan:

From January to mid-March 2003, the Turks really started a big campaign, claiming they were suffering from greatly increased attacks from the PKK. I saw it as a deliberate way for the Turks to come up with a pretext to invade and occupy Kurdistan, because if they could come up with a pretext to do that, it would have really made it impossible for us to liberate Kurdistan and Northern Iraq from Saddam.

A Turkish invasion would've enabled Saddam Hussein to keep an Arab jackboot on the necks of the Kurds, which the Turks saw as being in their best interest.

In January and February, the Turkish Army moved a lot of troops, and heavy mechanized infantry and tanks, toward the Turkey-Iraq border.

They made a lot of preparations for this. We really got into this dynamic where the Turks would lean real hard on the U.S. embassy in Ankara, and then the embassy would fire off a lot of message traffic to us, in Kurdistan, concerning the Turkish version of what was going on.

We were progressively being leaned on harder and harder, by Washington and Ankara, to make the KDP fix this problem.

Everyone in Washington was still desperate to get Turkish approval for 4th Infantry Division and 10th Group Special Forces to cross the border at Harburr and drive on to Mosul and liberate Northern Iraq.

Nothing the Turks had done, for over a year, could remotely suggest that they'd allow U.S. troops to go into Iraq from Turkey, however. So, the Turks kept pitching a fit about the PKK, and Washington was just desperate.

Bush was leaning on us to get the Kurds to fix the PKK problem, and meanwhile, the Turks were moving troops to the border and screaming that they would invade.

The Kurds were saying meaningful things in response to the Turkish threats to invade, like, "Last man standing. We will fight the Turks to the death. Bring them on; Saddam fought us with a modern army and fighter jets and could not defeat us. We will eat roots. We will drink water from mountain streams. With my Kalashnikov, I can fight the Turks. If we run out of ammunition, we will throw rocks and boulders at the Turks, and fight them with spears and knives and our bare hands. We will not be defeated and we will not be destroyed. Tell Ankara to bring a lot of body bags."

This whole thing was just escalating, spiraling out of control. And the Kurds continued to fight fiercely against Al-Qaeda and Ansar al-Islam, especially near the Iranian border.

At this point, then, we decided, okay, since the Turks won't believe the Kurds and the Kurds won't believe the Turks, we'll find a way. We told our chief of station in February 2003, "You have the Turks tell you exactly where these PKK bases are in northern Kurdistan, where the Turks claim the Kurds are harboring PKK. We will dispatch a counterterrorist team. We will physically go on the ground in Kurdistan where the Turks claim there are PKK. One of two things will happen: We will find them and destroy them, or we will not find them. If the PKK are at the ten-digit grids where the Turks say they are, then we will destroy them."

We offered to take the Turks with us. "Jump in the Land Cruiser with us, and you can report on this directly to Turkish General Staff. Lock and load. How much better can it get for you than this?" But they refused. The Turks refused to roll with us and strike at the PKK.

So, we sent our team, four to six guys, couple of Land Cruisers, and it was a big drain on counterterrorism resources.

We didn't find a single PKK at any of the ten-digit grids in Kurdistan that the Turkish General Staff had provided.

Meanwhile, a big black cloud shadowing us from Turkey was threatening to derail the whole invasion of Iraq: All of our resupply came from Incirlik, and the Turks, from jump street, had denied us air resupply, and, of course, air of any kind.

We could not get air support on missions.

The guys from Incirlik would meet us at the gate at Harburr. We'd dispatch a team from Salahuddin with trucks, go to Harburr, and transfer everything from their trucks to our trucks, and then drive it all back to Salahuddin.

It became really problematic for clandestine and counterterrorist ops, every time we did that.

And the roads were treacherous in the winter. Logistically, it was a huge problem that caused greater operational problems.

Every time we had to resupply our teams, we had to get permission from the Turkish General Staff, well in advance—ten days to two weeks—and it all had to be signed off on by Turkish General Staff. The guys in Incirlik had to get the permission, and it's more complicated than just getting the okay from the Turkish General Staff. There was more than one Turkish center of gravity.

The Turkish Special Forces commander in Silopi, not far from the border, had responsibility for Harburr. He was not happy that we were in Kurdistan, at all. Throughout the deployment, he looked for every opportunity to give us a hard time.

So, we had this real cumbersome procedure, weeks-in-advance permission to resupply. And physically, it was a really difficult thing to do, even with authorization. We brought in only the stuff we couldn't find locally.

We fed ourselves completely off the local economy. The only food we brought in was MREs for field operations.

The supply situation was so bad that on many occasions, we purchased satellite phones and computers in Kurdistan. Headquarters wasn't happy about that, but we told them, "We've got a job to do, and the Turks aren't helping us do it."

The boiling point came during this time, January to March 2003, when the Turks denied us weapons, ammunition, explosives, and food coming across the border, into Iraq.

So, we started procuring weapons from the Kurds: Kalashnikov 7.62 assault rifles and Heckler & Koch 9mm Mp5 submachine guns.

Headquarters gave me a ration of shit: They just went batshit crazy about this, explaining it to me this way: "You, Sam, do not have the legal authority to procure weapons. If you want these weapons, you have to submit a request and send it back here. If it is determined that you have a real need for a weapon, then at that point, we will procure it and send it to you."

This is sixteen months after September 11th in a war zone in which Al-Qaeda and Ansar al-Islam are targeting us. And we were right in Al-Qaeda's backyard.

So, we went to the Kurds and they got us the weapons.

We took the weapons and gave them cash.

And we told the Kurds, "I just want you to know, for the record, that I am not buying these weapons from you. I am just *renting* these weapons. When I am done with them, I will give them back to you. Consider the money as a loan that you don't have to pay back."

The Kurds were completely boggled by this. We had the most tortuous conversation with the KDP, on the weapons we needed: "But Sam, these are your weapons now," the KDP told me. "You can keep them. You bought them."

"No, my Kurdish brother, we cannot use the word *buy,* or any derivation of that verb. Just say *rent,* Mohammed, just say *rent.*"

"But no one rents weapons! These are yours, now. Keep them."

Now, at the time we were doing this, we were having so much trouble with the Turks, who began to physically inspect everything we brought across.

Turkish Army, in uniform at the U.S. Air Force Base in Incirlik, demanded the right to physically inspect every object we brought across.

So, on several occasions, we had replacements arrive in-country, and the Turks would not let them bring their weapons.

We actually had case officers and counterterrorist officers entering a war zone without any weapons at all to protect and defend themselves. This is sixteen, seventeen, and eighteen months after September 11th, in Al-Qaeda's backyard. We had guys showing up unarmed and, simultaneously, trying to acquire weapons for the team in-country, and getting this nonsensical feedback from Washington.

In the interests of trying to get us resupplied, the people in Incirlik had to take a lot of grief from the Turkish Army.

The Turks stalled when we'd apply for permission to resupply.

It would be weeks in between runs to the border. The Turks were not happy at all that we'd stayed, and the closer we got to invasion, the unhappier the Turks got.

It got worse as the winter went by and we neared March.

At the border, the Turks ransacked our gear and supplies. The Turks declared that our communications gear and weapons were forbidden from moving from Incirlik to us at the border.

The guys at Incirlik told us throughout the winter that the Turks did not allow our weapons, ammunition, explosives, and communications gear on our resupply convoys. On some occasions, we went to the border and the convoy would be there, waiting for us, but the Turkish Army at Harburr would not allow our resupply convoys to cross because they would claim that the guys in Incirlik had not filed the correct paperwork.

The Turkish Army at the border became increasingly more hostile and abusive toward us.

The guys were having a hard time avoiding a confrontation.

Roger that; we were well armed, and so were the Turks. The Turkish soldiers verbally abused my team, treating them like servants, and there were some very heated exchanges and tense moments at the border. As this went on, our guys had been working, minimum eighteen hours days, seven days a week, and there is no rear area.

Our counterterrorists were constantly targeted by Al-Qaeda and Ansar al-Islam cells, and Saddam's *Mukhabarat* made numerous assassination attempts against us.

With all the resupply headaches caused by the Turks, we had to scrounge to keep counterterrorism operations going.

As the months went by, we were literally at the point where the threads were coming out of our trousers and the tread was worn off our boots, and there was no way to replace them, from Incirlik.

So, we looked for clothes and boots in markets in Kurdistan.

I had laptop computers, part of our communications package, going down. And in order to keep CIA communications working, I had to send some of my team into Erbil to get parts from local computer shops, all part of the local economy.

How ugly did it get with the Turks at the border? Pretty damn ugly.

The worst incident with the Turks was when they threatened to arrest one of our senior officers.

A senior clandestine field officer came in from CIA headquarters to take a look at our operation in mid-February 2003. He spent two weeks in-country, at Salahuddin and Qal'ah Chulan, to get eyes on and really see how things were working on the ground. He was the only senior officer who made that trip during the entire deployment.

This clearly bothered the Turkish General Staff and Turkish Army—that he was on the ground in Kurdistan. I presume it bothered the Turks that a senior-level clandestine field officer was going to have discussions with the Kurdish leadership on the ground in Kurdistan. His reason for coming, however, was to get ground truth on our operation.

After his arrival, we were told by the Turks in Kurdistan and Ankara: "We insist on sitting in on all the meetings the senior U.S. clandestine officer has with the Kurds. And by the way, this is what we agreed to when we gave you Americans permission to cross the border into Kurdistan."

I was talking to the senior officer the morning we received this notification in Salahuddin. We showed him the message traffic from Ankara.

Not only were the Turks claiming we'd agreed to their demands on this earlier, but they also claimed that the officer had personally agreed to the same demands.

As he read the message, the officer looked at me and said, "What is this all about? I never agreed to such a thing. There was no discussion at all between me and the Turks about any such condition." He was incredulous.

I said, "Welcome to our world. That's how things work here. The Turks just dream up any objection and any way to fuck with us, at any time, twenty-four/seven, night and day."

Upon reflection, the guy who was really furious about our senior clandestine field officer being on the ground in Kurdistan was the Turkish Special Forces general in Silopi. The Turkish demands continued: "You will allow us into the meeting with the Kurds. It will happen. You Americans will do this, now."

And we kept telling the Turks, "Welcome to Groundhog Day. You can ask as many times as you want, but it ain't gonna happen."

So, finally we had this wonderfully surreal moment when a Turkish lieutenant came to one of our meetings in Salahuddin and said, "The Turkish Special Forces commander at Silopi has ordered me to tell you that when your senior clandestine field officer crosses back into Turkey, the Turkish Army will arrest him at Harburr."

We looked at this Turkish lieutenant and said, "Are you kidding? You are going to arrest a senior U.S. government official—that's what you are saying. Are you mad?"

The lieutenant replied, "The general has said that this will happen, and it *will* happen. We will arrest this man when he comes back into Turkey."

This was all within a couple days of when the CIA's most senior clandestine field officer in the Near East at that time was supposed to leave Kurdistan, cross into Turkey at Harburr, and leave Ankara for Washington.

Sam talked to him about staying in Salahuddin, but the field officer said, "No, I'll chance it." The Turkish Army's standing order to arrest the CIA's senior clandestine field officer at Harburr did not change.

Nobody helped Sam and his team on this, not even CIA headquarters.

Sam went to the Turkish border at Harburr with the CIA's senior clandestine field officer in the Near East. He took all of his shooters, armed to the teeth.

If the Turkish Army at Harburr had laid hands on him, Sam and his team planned to save the CIA senior clandestine field officer, and take him back into Kurdistan.

As Sam said in Philadelphia four years later, as Diana Krall sang "Only the Lonely" while a cold December wind scattered golden and red leaves down streets near the Delaware River:

> We would not allow our NATO ally, Turkey, to arrest our senior clandestine field officer, and our safe haven from the Turks was, of course, Kurdistan.
>
> The Kurds were the only friends we had.
>
> We got to the border, crossed it, and went into Harburr.
>
> I was afraid that the Turks were indeed going to arrest him and that there was a real chance that some of our guys, and no doubt some Turkish soldiers, were going to get killed.

But by being there, I reckoned that I'd have a chance to stop that from happening, and have some control over the situation.

And I told the Turks in Salahuddin the day before, "The reason I am going to Harburr is that I will not allow our senior clandestine field officer to be arrested by the Turkish Army. That is not going to happen."

I wanted the Turks in Salahuddin to telegraph to the Turkish General Staff and to the Turkish Army at Harburr and Silopi, "This is going to be ugly; if you attempt to arrest the U.S. senior clandestine field officer, it is not going to be a walk in the park. The Americans will not allow the Turkish Army to arrest their senior clandestine field officer. End of transmission."

And this was all happening when the Bush White House was still mainlining Cheney's heroin in Washington and smiling and saying, "Oh yes, the Turks are going to allow 4th ID and 10th Group to cross at Harburr, and our choppers will be flying out of Incirlik, no worries. The Turks are our beloved NATO ally and they will come through for us."

The Turkish Army did not arrest our senior clandestine field officer, thank God. The Turks blinked, and we had a team drive him on to Ankara.

I'd asked him if he wanted us to guard him all the way back to Ankara. He replied, "Many thanks, but it appears that someone talked sense to the Turkish Special Forces general in Silopi. I should be okay now. Steer clear of the *Mukhabarat,* and, gentlemen, stay healthy."

He was aware of Saddam's *Mukhabarat* and their attempted assassinations of me and my team. Again, had the Kurds not helped us at every opportunity from January to March 2003, God only knows where we would've ended up.

Kurdish aid was crucial to our survival.

As we carried out more clandestine missions, we ran increasingly large numbers of assets at a breakneck pace.

We were fully conscious that if you move at this kind of pace, you are going to pick up a lot of dust. And dust leaves a trail.

So, you're talking to a guy who is telling you about Saddam's Republican Guard, and you've met him once or twice. You know almost nothing about this guy. Who is he—why is he there?

And you're having a hard time verifying that what he is telling you is true. We were aware of the danger of being targeted by Saddam's *Mukhabarat* before entering Iraq, and having the Iraqis attempt to assassinate us—that was on our mind, all the time.

As we ran more assets during the winter of 2003, we determined conclusively that the Iraqis were definitely trying to kill us.

At first, what we got a lot of, from different sources, was, "The Iraqis are aware that there are Americans in the north. They are trying to find out who you are and what you are doing in the north." The *Mukhabarat*'s information, as far as we could tell, was really bad.

Saddam never really figured out who we were, exactly. The *Mukhabarat* thought that we were some kind of U.S. Special Operations force. They also had really exaggerated ideas of how many of us there were. They thought that there were, literally, five hundred of us. Which was fine with us.

So, as we detected and detained the *Mukhabarat*'s assets, they began a very concerted effort to position themselves to ambush and kill us. They started sending Iraqis to talk to us, feeding us real information, and once they got us to a point where we'd trust them, they would bring other people into the picture.

The *Mukhabarat* thought that they would get us to agree to meet them in places where they could dictate and control the meetings. Either they would ambush us with small arms, or kill us with a car bomb, or kill us at the meeting.

I knew an Iraqi Kurd, in particular, who had told us that he was going to bring us to a meeting with several other Iraqis. He was a Kurdish *jahahyshee,* a traitor, and he was in Saddam's government. I called him JoJo.

JoJo wanted to bring two *Mukhabarat* officers to kill us. We knew, independently, that the *Mukhabarat* were going to try to develop trust and then get us in an operation with them. Their goal was to meet us in a location that they could control, and kill at least eight of my guys at one time.

I disagreed with one of our case officers on this. He wanted to break contact and walk away, which is a school solution.

I said, "Disappear the textbook; we're not going to leave these *Mukhabarat* guys out there in Kurdistan, because they will then come up with new ways to kill us. Maintain contact.

"Tell JoJo to bring his boys. Tell him everything is cool."

Roger that; we sent JoJo the message. So, JoJo went out and got his *Mukhabarat* and we met them at a safe house in Erbil.

We searched everyone before they came in. They were unarmed, and they told us their fabulous story, that they represented "the brave Arab dissidents inside Iraq who are ready to end the era of evil Saddam!"

We deliberately let the meeting go on for a couple of reasons: One, we were interested in seeing how they structured their story; and two, to have fun.

We had lots of tea and handed them cartons of cigarettes and told the *Mukhabarat,* "We can't wait for you to take down Saddam."

Then, we stood up and opened a wide door for them to leave, and a half-dozen of our shooters were standing there with their M4s at combat ready, and one of our Special Operations commandos said to the first *Mukhabarat* officer, "Come with me, motherfucker."

One second, they were convinced they had pulled off the greatest coup, and the very next second, they were getting cuffed and yelled at.

And since we had KDP *peshmerga* outside, our guys took them out of the safe house and handed them over to the Kurds.

On three other occasions, we used assets, set up the meetings in locations we could control, and then captured the *Mukhabarat* assassination teams.

The dominant reaction of the *Mukhabarat* hit teams was relief. They didn't start singing and dancing, but they were not unhappy. This was the perfect resolution for them; they didn't have to kill anybody, and Saddam's guys couldn't really target their families, since they'd been captured on operations for Saddam, and they could sit out the war.

The *Mukhabarat* never stopped sending hit teams, all winter.

One of the last cases we worked, the *Mukhabarat* decided to offer a bounty in late February 2003.

They put a bounty on the heads of all Americans in Northern Iraq: "Kill or capture."

Saddam really thought the *Mukhabarat* would stamp us.

Saddam wanted to capture an American and put him on trial in Baghdad, get CNN and BBC world coverage, and so on, and then hang him.

Saddam really knew how to hustle the Western media, how to play the media game, and he was very eager to put on a show.

There was an asset we had, a double agent, being run by a *Mukhabarat* officer in Northern Iraq. We used the asset and set up a meeting with the *Mukhabarat* officer.

The *Mukhabarat* agreed to be turned and go to work for us.

So, he was working for the commander of all *Mukhabarat* in Northern Iraq, who was in Mosul.

And the guy we turned was a lieutenant colonel in the *Mukhabarat,* and from the Mosul office. The *Mukhabarat* was getting massive pressure from Saddam, personally: He wanted an American to parade around for the world press.

We told the lieutenant colonel, "We are tired of them waiting to target us. Let's turn this all around." We used him to lure even more *Mukhabarat* into Kurdistan, and started reeling them in.

We had to make it look like he was having significant success.

We took one of our guys and put him in military uniform, which our Special Forces commandos had in their duffel bags. We had him lay in a ditch on the side of a mountain road, with ketchup all over him, and took some cheesy photographs.

And we had the *Mukhabarat* lieutenant colonel send these photos back to Mosul, with the message, "I am having great success—I've killed one of the American Special Forces commanders! He was a U.S. Army Special Forces colonel!"

The Mosul office of *Mukhabarat* bought this, forwarded it to Saddam, and Saddam and the *Mukhabarat* were ecstatic.

Mosul replied: "This is great. You've killed the high-ranking American Special Operations commander! Magnificent! But what would really be great is if you could get one alive. Now, get one alive and bring him to Mosul, and we will take him to Saddam. Saddam wants him in Baghdad."

"Absolutely," our double agent said. "But to do that, you need to send me a team. With a team of *Mukhabarat* officers, I can capture at least one American alive."

They exchanged messages by courier, and at some point, the Mosul *Mukhabarat* commander wanted a cell-phone conversation with our double agent.

We set up the call so we could listen in. You could *almost* feel sorry for that *Mukhabarat* colonel in Mosul. You could hear exactly what was going on in his head. He desperately wanted to pull this off and be a great hero, which would get Baghdad, and Saddam, off his ass.

On the other hand, you could also hear that he was not an idiot: The longer he talked to our asset, the more you could hear him gradually coming to the conclusion that this all sounded too good to be true.

He was a pro at intelligence. At the end of the conversation, he laid out all the arrangements to send a *Mukhabarat* team near Erbil.

But as soon as we hung up the phones, our case officer, who speaks perfect Arabic, said, "He ain't coming. He's figured out exactly that you," he said, pointing to our asset, "are no longer on Saddam's team."

Our case officer was right; that line went completely dead. We never heard from the *Mukhabarat* in Mosul again.

But they heard from us.

We started sending Kurdish teams everywhere on the other side of the Green Line after March 18, 2003, including Mosul, of course.

And it turned out that the KDP already had an asset who had penetrated the Northern Iraq headquarters of the *Mukhabarat,* in Mosul.

The Kurds had a spy inside the Northern Iraq headquarters of Saddam's *Mukhabarat,* 100 percent. He had physical access to the *Mukhabarat* northern headquarters, on all floors.

So, to repay the favor for all the times that the *Mukhabarat* had tried to kill us, we had a team build a satchel charge in a briefcase, which our Kurdish asset took into Mosul.

He put it on the ground floor of the *Mukhabarat* headquarters and left the building. It blew the shit out of most of that building, and fire destroyed the rest of it. After all the decades of Saddam's *Mukhabarat* in Mosul, it was ultimately a Kurd who struck and killed *Mukhabarat* in the very building that they had used to plan and execute the al-Anfal operations from 1987 to 1989, when Saddam had ordered the widespread torture, rape, and murder of 180,000 Kurds.

Where the Kurds really showed their patience and faith in us—when very little on the ground gave them any reason for faith in the Bush administration and the U.S. government—was starting in mid-January 2003, regarding weapons. In mid-January, we got communications from headquarters that, finally, we were going to give the Kurds ammunition, mortar rounds, and weapons.

We began the familiar dialogue with Washington: "How are you going to bring in the weapons for the Kurds when the Turks allow no air transit?"

"Oh, we're going to fly them in."

To which we'd say, "Ah, we don't have a plane, and the Turks won't let you fly anything in to us. And you've known that for nearly a year."

Their response: "We're having ongoing discussions with the Turks, and we expect that we are going to have Turkish approval by such and such a date."

Quite frankly, the dates appeared completely random to us. For example, we'd ask headquarters, "When's the flight coming?" and they'd say, "It's coming in five days." We'd say, "How's that possible, because the Turks haven't given any approval?"

This is the same time that we couldn't get anything across the border by land, including food, ammunition, and weapons, and the Turks would only allow new guys on our team to enter Iraq if they were combat-naked—without a weapon.

Headquarters would say, "Chief of Station has a meeting with somebody, and we hope to have approval, then, for planes coming in."

This is a reflection of the familiar dynamic of Bush being divorced from reality. Headquarters was being thumped on the head by the White House: "We've gotta go to war in Iraq! And you've gotta arm the Kurds, and that means you, CIA, have to get weapons into Iraq."

So, we had these communications with headquarters, and the Chief of Station had his meeting, and of course the Turks did not give their approval.

By now, in my communications with headquarters, it was no holds barred: "This just does not work. Everything about this operation is fucked. From day one, we have never gotten any of the support you promised us. Whether it's air, whether it's weapons for the Kurds, gas masks, you name it—you guys have not been able to hold up your end of the bargain. Everything we're doing on the ground here has been accomplished *despite* the fact that you have completely dropped the ball on your end."

The proposed weapons flights were all scheduled prior to the arrival of 10th Group Special Forces in Kurdistan. And the intensity of the "We're Going to War" mantra from the White House increased dramatically; a big drum beating in the background of the entire operation, by mid-January, it was just deafening.

Now, for the first time, CIA headquarters was saying, "You need to prepare for the possibility that 10th Group is not coming."

Sam and his team were hearing that the two main bases, Salahuddin and Qal'ah Chulan, with a total of seventy CIA and U.S. Special Operations forces, would be on point for the Iraq War. The seventy Americans were facing off against 150,000 Iraqi troops—the whole Northern front of the Iraqi Army.

Sam said to headquarters, "So, what I'm hearing from you is that I should start preparing for the possibility that we are going to war, and it is us and the Kurds against 150,000 Iraqi Army troops and the *Mukhabarat,* the entire Northern Front of the Iraqi Army." The guy I was talking to from Iraqi Operations Group paused. There was a long silence, and then he replied, "Yes."

In response to Bush providing no plan of attack on the Iraqi Army in Northern Iraq, Sam and his team put together a plan to defend the entire Green Line against the Iraqi Army.

Effectively, it meant that the Americans and Kurds would be linked up, along the Green Line and deep in the mountains of Kurdistan. Sam, coordinating with Masrour Barzani, General Mustafa Amin, and other high-ranking *peshmerga* commanders, set up a fallback base in Shaqlawa.

We took over a small hotel and equipped it with water and generators.

We bought tanker trucks full of gasoline and set up our own fuel depot, in anticipation of fuel being cut off.

We had rooms full of cases of bottled water. What we knew, moreover, was that if the war started as things stood, the Iraqis may very well have gone on the offensive, meaning that our existing escape route would be cut. That's the way the war would begin for us—losing our supplies and our way out. No way we could drive back across the Harburr River, and no way we could get supplies in.

We scouted out an escape route due north, through the mountains.

We would drive as far as we could on hardtop roads, and take the Land Cruisers on back roads and jeep trails, and then abandon all the vehicles and walk with our rucks through the mountains.

Then, we'd construct a rope bridge over a river into Turkey. And by the way, we would have had no permission to be in Turkey.

Strangely enough, before I ever left America, when still at headquarters in spring 2002, I had this strange feeling that it might be a good idea to know how to escape from Kurdistan into Turkey.

I talked to an analyst, who is an expert on the Near East and knows Turkey very well. I asked him, "What's the closest Turkish *gendarme* post, due north, from Salahuddin?"

He rummaged around a landslide of papers and pulled out a map. On the map, he had marked the exact locations, the ten-digit grids, of every *gendarme* post. I looked at one specific post, and took the ten-digit grids, and before I left America, I put them in my GPS.

I called that post *Cayhane,* which means "tea house" in Turkish, because if we had to escape, I wanted to stay alive long enough to drink tea at that *gendarme* post in Turkey. That was my way home.

I also brought an American flag. The plan was for me to raise the flag on a pole and show it in Turkey. That was our grandiose escape plan, since no one could assist us in any fashion, otherwise.

Even in our evacuation plans, we were on our own. We could not expect anything from anybody else. After all the hassles, headaches, and nearly throwing down at the border with the Turkish Army, there was no way I could count on the American NATO ally Turkey, should we have had to escape into Turkey.

The plan to supply weapons to the Kurds went from the god-awful to the Twilight Zone.

In late January, headquarters told us, "The planes are coming, Aleutian 76s flown by contract pilots, old Russian planes, carrying all these weapons for the Kurds. You've got to get the airfield at Hareer ready now; light up the field, bring in all the aircraft, unload all these aircraft of many tons of ordnance."

I told headquarters, "Look, that means forklifts. That means cargo trucks. And we don't have a logistical base."

Washington didn't understand that Hareer is not a U.S. military air base where all of this would be on hand. The only thing that existed at Hareer was an airstrip in the middle of a field of high grass.

So, I asked headquarters, "What has changed? How are you going to fly these aircraft here from Turkey?" Headquarters, once again: "Oh, we are going to get Turkish approval. Trust us, it's fixed."

To say the least, I was extremely skeptical. But headquarters gave me direct orders, at that point: "Get the Kurds and get it done. Light up the airfield. Get the forklifts and cargo trucks." So, we got it done. We went and told Masrour, and he was ecstatic. All the Kurds were ecstatic. We put together a team and lit up the field and got the forklifts and cargo trucks.

The planes didn't come.

Our credibility with the Kurds, which was already on life support, was now really hurting. Our guys were just fucking furious. "Are you kidding me? After a year, headquarters still can't get its act together."

Headquarters then told us, sheepishly, "Well, the Turks didn't give their approval." Roger that. Why was I not surprised?

A few days later, headquarters told us to do it again. We did the whole goddamned thing again. And once again, the Turks didn't give their approval.

The Kurds were disgusted and my guys were livid. Just outraged, that we were making the Kurds go through these incredible gyrations to help us, with 150,000 Iraqi Army across the Green Line, and the *Mukhabarat,* Al-Qaeda, and Ansar al-Islam still trying to kill us.

Every day we were dealing with people trying to kill us, and our route to safety was, "Put on your ruck and walk home."

We were maintaining our relationship with the Kurds based purely on personal relationships and personal trust. So, after the second loss of face, we took another step into the Twilight Zone.

Washington now acknowledged that they had no reasonable prospect in the near term of getting the Turks to approve overflight, which we'd known for a year.

This whole adventure started in the first place when the Turks refused us permission to land in Turkey in July 2002. Now Washington acknowledged this and came up with a series of incredibly bizarre proposals for how they claimed they would get Turkish approval to get the planes in.

For example, at one point they told me, "We will fly the planes directly down the border, between Turkey and Iran. Since it will be right on the border, it won't be Turkish airspace, and that's how we'll get them in. They will fly the border down, and get into Iraq that way."

I replied, "If you're flying on the border between Turkey and Iran, and you're not in Turkey anymore, then you must be in Iran. And you don't have approval to fly over Iran, do you?"

They said, "No, but maybe if it is only a couple of miles into Iranian airspace, the Iranians won't mind."

"I have a suspicion that the Iranians look at this equation a little differently than you do," I told headquarters. "Good luck."

The next idea they came up with was that they would fly over Syrian airspace, with an escort of U.S. fighters to clear the airspace over Syria.

"What are you talking about?" I asked headquarters. "We're not at war with Syria. We're not trying to go to war with Syria. No way in hell that anyone in the U.S. Air Force, or any other branch of the U.S. military, is going to order anyone to shoot Syrian planes down when the Syrians are acting in self-defense. And once U.S. fighters enter Syrian airspace, by all justification of international law, the Syrians are going to defend their airspace."

The last idea they had was my personal favorite. They had determined that international airspace only extends up to between 60,000 and 70,000 feet.

So, they were going to have the aircraft go up to 70,000 feet and fly over Syria, in that fashion, and then dive down into Hareer airfield in Kurdistan.

"I'm sorry, but are you trying to tell me that you are going to resupply us from outer space?" I asked the Iraq Operations Group. "Does it matter that the Aleutian 76s don't fly at 70,000 feet? You're talking about private aircraft that you are going to contract, old Russian IL-76s; God only knows what they have been through. Whatever their maximum ceiling when they were first manufactured, which doesn't begin to approach sixty to seventy thousand feet, it's only a fraction of that now."

I remember that when I got off the phone, one of my team leaders asked, "Is that true—that international airspace doesn't exist above sixty thousand feet?"

I told him, "I don't know, and I don't care, because you and I both know they are not going to do it."

At this stage, we were having serious discussions about the very real possibility that the Kurds would lay it on the line with us: "You know what, guys—we don't want to go to this party with you, after all."

Obviously, the Kurds wanted to get rid of Saddam. On the other hand, the Kurds were not doing so badly since the Green Line had been drawn up and enforced by the United Nations. And up to this point, the only thing the Kurds had seen Bush do was fail to come through on any promises he'd made in 2002.

In Asian terms—and we were in Asia, dealing with Asians . . . Asians named Kurds and Arabs— Bush had already lost face miserably by February 2003, in Kurdistan, Southwest Asia.

There was never any guarantee here that the Kurds were going to participate. Washington may have assumed that, but that was a very dangerous assumption.

Bush wouldn't give the Kurds 300,000 gas masks, but was talking all kinds of shit to the Kurds and the rest of the world about how he was going to kick Saddam's ass.

The flights to support the Kurds never came. Ever. The first U.S. aircraft to land in Northern Iraq showed up after the 173rd dropped from the sky. Nothing ever came for us and the Kurds in January or February—actually, not until March.

Six more times, headquarters told us that we needed to set up the airfield and offload supply flights for the Kurds.

On each of those six occasions, I did not tell the Kurds nor did I tell my team. I figured it was on my head if it went wrong.

And I stood down each order from Washington on those six occasions—I did not tell headquarters. Had those six flights landed, I would've been in deep kimchi, but I knew that none of them would land.

And dragging the Kurds out six more times, after the initial incredible loss of face on the first two no-shows, would've destroyed our relationship with the Kurds. Thank God we stood down from trotting the Kurds out, because we would've lost face six more times, and that would've ended Kurdish support for us, and any future commitment from them. There is no way that we could have continued losing face to the Kurds and remained in-country.

I have to think that internally, the Kurds must have had some very serious conversations about whether we were really going to finish the job, or whether they should just tell us to leave.

Certainly, previous U.S. governments had hung the Kurds out to dry, in 1975 and in 1991, and that was no doubt on the minds of senior Kurdish leadership in Kurdistan—that Bush might hang them out to dry again in 2002–2003.

Meanwhile, Washington sent a three-man Marine team into Kurdistan in February 2003.

Major General Osman, who is now a lieutenant general, led the team. His intelligence officer was Colonel Lawless, a full-bird colonel and a real intelligence professional. His ops guru was a great Marine senior staff noncommissioned officer, Master Gunnery Sergeant McPherson. McPherson is very sharp, analytical, and matter-of-fact.

The Marines were sent in to try to deal with what was expected to be a post-invasion Kurdish refugee crisis, given Saddam's previous use of chemical weapons.

The Turks, however, decided to hassle Major General Osman, who had to get permission from the Turkish General Staff to enter Kurdistan. Without a weapon.

He was allowed to bring along a very limited communications package, but no weapons. That is correct: The Marines were in uniform, in a war zone, where Al-Qaeda, Ansar al-Islam, the *Mukhabarat*, and 150,000 Iraqi Army soldiers would've been happy to kill them. And the Turks said, "We don't care, Major General; you and your Marines will not enter Iraq with any weapons."

We got a heads-up from Washington, an "oh, by the way," that the Marine team was coming, but we were not ordered to make contact with them or to help them.

And they had no instructions to lash up with us, nor any mechanism; they didn't even know our location or how to meet us. I looked at this message and decided, "We've got this Marine general and his team on the ground over here; we need to go find them and help them out."

The Kurds had brought them in from Zakho, and we reached out to the Kurds and found out that they were in Salahuddin.

I rolled up to their guesthouse, which was guarded by Kurdish *peshmerga*. The Marine team was trying to make their very limited, unsophisticated, rudimentary communications gear work.

It turned out that the Turkish Army at Harburr had denied them all of their state-of-the-art communications gear. That's correct; the Turks grabbed their gear at the border.

We walked in and said, "Welcome to Kurdistan. We are the guys from the CIA. What can we do to help you?"

They were a little freaked out. All they knew, prior to us meeting them, was that we were somewhere in Kurdistan.

That's all they had been told. Don't get me wrong: These were three of the most impressive guys I have ever met in my life, and we developed quite a solid relationship with the Marines, even though it wasn't our job.

When the shooting war started in March, we campaigned with our headquarters to put Major

General Osman in charge of all Coalition forces in Northern Iraq.

He never asked us to do that, and I don't know that he was even aware that we did it, since we did so on our own secure communications. Coalition operations started in Northern Iraq in March 2003, without a U.S. general in command, and we kept saying to our headquarters, "Look, you have a Marine major general here who is brilliant. He understands all the political, cultural, and military dynamics on the ground here; why don't you put him in charge?"

But nothing ever happened with any of that—another example of Washington refusing to trust field intelligence.

The Marine team told us about their communications problem, most of it due to lack of hardware. I told them, "I've got a base right down the road, with all kinds of communications gear and experienced communicators. Why don't I bring my communicators over here and have them fix your problem?" They told us about their immediate need to send messages and I said, "No worries; I'll drive you over to our base and you can send the traffic, ASAP."

Next, the Marines told me, "Look, the Turks denied us weapons. We need weapons and ammunition."

I replied, "How about we take you up to the base, you tell me what weapons you need, and we will issue you weapons and ammunition, right now."

I remember very vividly what Lawless said next, poker-faced: "Outstanding. You know what—I could really use a good cup of coffee, too."

Lawless and McPherson came with us, to our base. Walking into our base house, to get to the kitchen, you had to walk through the front door and through a common room.

One of our counterterrorists had managed to get a PlayStation hooked up in the common room, and he was playing *Grand Theft Auto*. Three guys were chilling out on a sofa nearby, watching *Sideways* on a DVD player and telling him, "Dude, you're a loser on PlayStation."

Stacked against the wall were rucks and long rifles, and everyone had a sidearm. Meanwhile, we had guys going out a side door, all gunned up, ready to go on a mission, and our Kurdish staff was hustling around, handing out cold sodas, singing Kurdish songs.

The whole scene was kind of like a cross between a frat house, a Kurdish fiesta, a clandestine safe house, and a military camp, all in one.

We took Lawless into the kitchen and I told one of our Kurdish staff to get him a coffee; she wasn't keen on fixing the coffee since it was so late. Lawless and MacPherson glanced back at the common room and then looked at me. Their faces were saying, "This is about as far from the Marine Corps as we can imagine." We got Lawless the coffee after I convinced our Kurdish cook that coffee for the Marines was a good idea. Roger that; all Marines need tobacco, coffee, and whiskey to survive in a war zone.

I got one of my communicators, right away, and sent him back with Lawless and McPherson. We issued them all firearms, and squared them away with sidearms—including Major General Osman, who also got a sidearm that night. We were short on M4s. Remember: The Turks had been very committed to denying us weapons and ammunition.

From that point on, we had a fabulous relationship with the Marine team. We had very different approaches, but, fundamentally, the same core philosophy: "Whatever needs to get done, no bullshit, no bureaucracy; whatever needs to happen, do it now. Now means *now*, not in five minutes."

Whatever they needed, we gave it to them. They were three of the most professional guys I have ever met in my life.

Their level of competence was extraordinary. They asked questions, and they listened; they *really* listened. We had no authority to tell them what to do, and it was not our place. But they considered us a resource, and they wanted to hear what we had to say.

They had this revolutionary concept that we had acquired all this expertise that they should listen to, absorb, and take advantage of in March 2003. Respect is a two-way street, and the respect was real and deep.

Our conversations with Major General Osman were predicated on him having convictions, and an attitude that said, "Tell me what you think, and tell me the history on the ground on this. I need to hear your perspective and the ground truth, here." Lawless was his Intel guy, and it was his primary function to gather information. He spent huge amounts of time listening to and talking with my team.

Oddly, Bush sent an ambassador whose attitude on listening and gaining information in a war zone was completely the opposite of Major General Osman and the Marines.

At one point, Ambassador Khalilzad arrived and went down to Major General Osman's guesthouse.

The ambassador's entire attitude was, "I don't need you; you have nothing to give to me." Fundamentally, Ambassador Khalilzad did not listen to Major General Osman because he walked into that meeting convinced that Major General Osman had nothing of value to tell him. He was the senior U.S. diplomat on the ground in Kurdistan and Northern Iraq, and he had no interest in listening to us, either.

The few occasions when Khalilzad did see us, he talked *at* us, not with us. He told us what the situation was in Kurdistan and Northern Iraq. Literally, we did not get a word in edgewise.

Every time I left a meeting with Ambassador Khalilzad, I left shaking my head, thinking, "This guy has no idea what is happening on the ground here, and he does not want to know what is happening on the ground here. He is one of the most arrogant pricks on the face of the planet; there is no one on earth who can tell him anything. He got on the plane stateside fully convinced that he knew everything he needed to know about Kurdistan and Northern Iraq, and once his plane landed in the Near East, he was still fully convinced."

Major General Osman was completely at the other end of the spectrum.

When we talked to Osman, it was clear that he was seeking out our field intelligence because he needed it in order to make a fully informed decision based on the actual reality on the ground in Kurdistan and Northern Iraq.

Osman, unlike Khalilzad, didn't get on a plane stateside with the attitude, "I already know everything I need to know about what's going down on the ground in Kurdistan and Northern Iraq."

Our relationship with Major General Osman and the Marine team paid off, for all of us. In early March 2003, there was a lot of hysteria getting picked up by the U.S. media, who declared that there was a humanitarian crisis: Hundreds of thousands of Kurds were without food and shelter in the mountains.

The heat came down on Osman from Washington regarding this media-orchestrated Kurdish refugee crisis. My team came up with a plan to sort this out and get the heat off the Marine team.

I ordered teams with digital cameras to visit and photograph every refugee camp. The photos showed camps that were 80 percent empty. We photographed every tent in every camp. The Kurds had been telling Washington directly, "There is no Kurdish refugee crisis," but the Bush administration refused to believe the Kurds. Washington was having a fit again, which was of no help to my team, the Marine team, or the Kurds. Washington wouldn't believe the Kurds, that there was no refugee crisis, so we stepped in and got the job done. That ended the hysteria in Washington, and the Marine team no longer had that distraction.

We began, at that point in early March, to create our own Kurdish *peshmerga* deep reconnaissance teams, which we trained and outfitted on our own. The Kurds were our only friends—well, the Kurds and the Marines, for sure.

"THE KURDS WERE BRILLIANT AND DID NOT FAIL US"

Kurdistan and Northern Iraq, March–May 2003

Kurdish *peshmerga* deep reconnaissance teams covertly penetrating across the Green Line were key to U.S. clandestine strategy beginning in the summer of 2002, when the Kurdish leadership shared their urgent concerns with Sam about an anticipated exodus from all of Kurdistan. This would come in the wake of expected chemical weapons attacks on Kurdish cities by Saddam's 400,000-strong Iraqi Army.

General Mustafa Amin, commanding general of all Kurdish Democratic Party *peshmerga* on the Green Line, in the Irbil sector, addressed those concerns directly in August 2002, asking Sam: "What is your plan when the Iraqi Army attacks Erbil with chemical weapons?"

Erbil is the heart of Kurdistan; home to half a million people, it is located only a few miles from the Green Line.

The Northern Front of the Iraqi Army, with a history of attacking Kurds with chemical weapons in our time, sat across the Green Line with 150,000 Iraqi Army soldiers.

The Kurds had firsthand experience with Saddam and his chemical weapons, and now they were concerned that Saddam would employ his surface-to-surface missiles as a chemical weapons delivery system.

Given what had happened in Kurdistan in 1987–1989, when tens of thousands of Kurds were massacred by the Iraqi Army and Iraqi Air Force with chemical agents, the Americans and the Kurds in Kurdistan in March 2003 were operating under the belief that Saddam would load up the Iraqi Army surface-to-surface missiles with chemical agents. Anthrax was also a major concern. Sam and his team had been told that Saddam had an anthrax capability, and the Americans got anthrax inoculations in early March 2003.

What the Kurds wanted from the Bush White House was an effective solution to the problem of stopping Saddam from attacking Kurdish cities with Iraqi chemical weapons.

Three blocks from the White House on a bitter cold, late-December afternoon in 2007, Sam thanked an Ethiopian waitress with a jet-black bob as she set Irish coffees on our table in a brick-walled bar. Sinatra was singing "The Lady is a Tramp" from a stereo behind the bar, and folks were laying down their gloves and scarves while Sam sipped his coffee and opened up about Saddam's threat to Kurdistan:

In March of 2003, Saddam's surface-to-surface missiles were at the top of our list of threats to our team, and threats to the Kurds. The Kurds were asking us every day, "How are you going to protect us from Saddam's surface-to-surface missiles?" We had made Washington aware of this constantly since July 2002. Washington had done nothing to resolve it, however.

The crux of the issue—what the Kurds had been saying to us since July 2002, and to Washington—was, "You, the United States, are going to begin this war; the very first thing that Saddam will do is fire these surface-to-surface missiles at our cities. Each missile will carry VX gas [nerve gas]. We've got Erbil, a city of a half-million people in Kurdistan, which will be barraged with chemical weapons by Saddam. How are you going to stop Saddam from doing that?"

Now it was March 2003, and the Kurds knew for a fact that we were going to war in Iraq. And nothing had changed from Washington, in terms of any plan to save the Kurds. In fact, there was no plan. Keep in mind: Washington had already decided, by March 2003, that we were not going to give gas masks to the Kurds.

Keeping the Kurds on board with the idea that the U.S. was actually going to war against Saddam was very problematic. Effectively, the Kurds said, "We want you to make it a top priority to track down and disable Saddam's surface-to-surface missiles."

We immediately relayed that to Washington, in early March 2003. The White House came back with, "Thanks for the input, but we are the White House, and we have our military plan for the Iraq War already. We have our list of targets, and just as gas masks for 300,000 Kurds is not a priority, neither is disabling Saddam's surface-to-surface missiles."

Washington was telling the Kurds, "You've got to line up with us, shoulder to shoulder, to take down Saddam, but we don't care that there are surface-to-surface missiles aimed at Kurdish cities by a brutal dictator who has never hesitated to slaughter Kurds with chemical weapons."

Washington was completely ignoring the historical reality once again. This was not a *theoretical* possibility for the Kurds. The Kurds had already lost untold thousands of people because of Saddam.

Washington was asking the Kurds to pretend like the history of Saddam's oppression of the Kurds had never happened.

So, we came up with a solution to this problem: ourselves. Deep reconnaissance teams. Kurds, trained in special operations, particularly long-range recon and demolitions. Their mission was to cross the Green Line and go deep into Iraqi territory, fifty to one hundred miles. Small teams of three to four *peshmerga* would hunt down and destroy surface-to-surface missiles. We equipped them with GPS, sidearms, Kalashnikovs, and ammunition. Their mission was to get ten-digit GPS grids on Saddam's surface-to-surface missiles, then call in air strikes on the missiles.

There were two pieces to this plan: The first was psychological; it was something we could do, along with the Kurds, to solve the problem. It showed the Kurds that we meant business, that we understood the threat to Kurdish cities. The second part was to find, fix, and destroy Iraqi forces, particularly Iraqi surface-to-surface missile units.

The real driving force here was that we understood we could not get Washington to commit to a change in strategy. No one inside the Beltway wanted to destroy Saddam's surface-to-surface missiles. We knew the only way to accomplish this was if we, ourselves, inside Iraq, could find a way to destroy them.

We found a way.

We knew the U.S. military would look at Saddam's surface-to-surface missiles as a direct threat to American lives, and not hesitate to destroy them. Beginning in January 2003, we selected Kurdish *peshmerga* in Salahuddin, screened them, and formed them into teams to carry out long-range reconnaissance and demolitions. Then, we trained them in the use of handheld GPS and satellite phones. We put together plans for infiltrating them all into Iraq.

We trained one hundred and fifty *peshmerga* for these deep reconnaissance teams. The training was very exacting and rigorous. Another critical point: All of this training was done by our team. Our 10th Group assets and our Agency assets were magnificent. Very thorough, very precise, and they communicated very well with the Kurds.

We sent our deep recon teams across the Green Line on March 15, 2003, seventy-two hours before the Air War started.

The Kurds started calling in locations, eventually calling in dozens and dozens of air strikes on Saddam's surface-to-surface missiles.

Roger that; the Kurds did not hesitate to throw down on Saddam.

We used our Kurdish deep recon teams to hunt, strike, and kill hundreds of targets; they were our only eyes and ears downrange, as there were no

Special Operations Forces in their area. A huge area, all of Northern Iraq beyond the Green Line, all the way to the Syrian and Turkish borders.

The Kurds were brilliant and did not fail us.

No doubt, the Iraqi Army's failure to strike at Kurdish cities had a lot to do with our Kurdish *peshmerga* deep recon teams who were hammering the Iraqi Army with air strikes. Saddam did not anticipate that, at all. Total stealth. We destroyed the missiles before he could launch them. And the strategic impact of our deep recon teams was significant.

Near Mosul, for instance, one of our four-man *peshmerga* deep recon teams caught an entire Iraqi Army mechanized infantry brigade that had pulled out of its position, moving south—probably the beginnings of a much larger movement by the Iraqi Army south. Our *peshmerga* deep recon team called in air strikes by the U.S. Navy on that Iraqi Army unit and obliterated it. That was the first and last time that the Iraqi Army tried to move a unit off the Northern Front.

The other thing that the *peshmerga* teams were extensively used for was hunting *Mukhabarat* and *feydayeen*. The U.S. military is not well suited when it comes to finding *Mukhabarat* and *feydayeen* rolling in different-colored BMWs. It takes real-time human Intel, not just aerial surveillance, to take down a mobile, camouflaged enemy. The *Mukhabarat* and *feydayeen* did not stay put. They were mobile.

Now, the ground war began, and we got all of this *feydayeen* violence, such as in Al-Nasiriyah, where the *feydayeen* became the main impediment.

We had never really considered the *feydayeen* to be a major target, or a major problem, before the ground war started. Frankly, we were pissed off.

We saw what the *feydayeen* were doing, countrywide, and since we had all the *peshmerga* teams downrange, we ordered them, "Find the *feydayeen*. Rules of engagement: Strike and kill the *feydayeen*." I remember telling one Kurdish deep recon team leader, "Kill the *feydayeen*. I want them dead."

The *feydayeen* moved as if they thought they were invisible, which was a mistake. For instance, the *feydayeen* would have a headquarters set up in a neighborhood in Mosul. Then, they'd set up safe houses.

We'd use our *peshmerga* teams to find the *feydayeen* headquarters and their safe houses, and we'd get real-time, eyes-on, human intelligence from our *peshmerga* teams, on the *feydayeen* locations in Mosul—and everywhere else.

Our *peshmerga* teams would then give us the ten-digit grids for each *feydayeen* location. We'd give the grids to U.S. military and they'd drop a JDAM bomb from high in the sky into the *feydayeen* headquarters in Mosul, and their safe houses.

And by the time the *feydayeen* set up a new headquarters in Mosul, our *peshmerga* teams would have discovered their locations and relayed the grids to us, and then we'd convince the *feydayeen* that we knew where they were, even from 35,000 feet. Our Kurdish *peshmerga* deep recon teams were very effective at killing *feydayeen* in March and April, 2003.

The *peshmerga* teams also struck at *Mukhabarat* in Northern Iraq.

One of the things that the Iraqis were very conscious of was our airpower and our technical intelligence capabilities—satellite, electronic Intel, etc. So, they believed that any fixed location they were at was going to be hit.

Now, every Iraqi organization had a plan to go mobile and displace. Typically, what it meant was moving into a building—a mosque, a private residence, anything that was not outwardly an official Iraqi government structure.

Like the Kurds, Sam knew that Saddam's secret police and internal security forces were committed to escaping the Zeus-like strength of U.S. and Coalition airpower, the waves of B-52s and B1B bombers and F-18 fighter bombers that would flood the skies over Iraq, once the Coalition began the invasion. Sam knew that long before March 2003, and he knew it applied to all Iraqi security services: the *feydayeen,* the *Mukhabarat,* the Special Security Organization, Military Intelligence, and a number of others, all under Saddam's thumb. Sam, like his team, also knew that Saddam designed redundancy into his dictatorship's secret police, at all levels, to militate against anyone creating a broad power base against him.

Inside Saddam's regime, nobody had their own fiefdom to develop a power base independent from Saddam, because if you could, then you'd have the potential to overthrow Saddam and the Baathists.

Only the Kurds had directly challenged Baathist rule, built a power base outside of Baghdad, and fought a guerrilla war against Saddam. With the fall of Saddam's Baathists in April 2003, the Kurds saw their dream from September 11, 1961, come true: the end of Arab rule over Kurdistan.

As Sam and the Kurds predicted, Baathist secret police and the *feydayeen* displaced when the first bombs struck Saddam's palace in Baghdad on March 18, 2003. Sam's Kurdish deep reconnaissance teams began hunting the *feydayeen* and *Mukhabarat,* and continued, also, carrying out sabotage missions against the Iraqi Army. As Sam said, ordering us a round of single malt scotch near the White House in early January 2008:

> Taking down the *Mukhabarat* was personal, as they'd been targeting us since July 2002, so our attitude was, "Gloves off—time to put you down so that you stay down." Roger that; the only dirty fight is the one you lose. Ulysses S. Grant understood that.
>
> There was a bigger strategic element involved in going after the *Mukhabarat* and *feydayeen:* We had been talking to hundreds and hundreds of Iraqi military, from privates to generals, since July 2002.
>
> But the Iraqi military deeply feared the *Mukhabarat;* they knew from past experience that if Saddam found out, through his security services, that they'd talked to an American—or any Westerner—Iraqi secret police would show up and disappear their families, and kill them also, of course.
>
> One key truth we nailed initially, talking to Iraqi military who clandestinely crossed the Green Line to meet us, was that the vast majority of the Iraqi Army had no desire to fight and die for Saddam.

Outside of a relatively small handful of individuals, every one of them wanted Saddam gone as much as we did. We got that from 95 percent of the Iraqi Army we contacted. The fundamental issue for the Iraqi Army was that they remained more afraid of Saddam than of us. They were not convinced that the United States was going to finish off Saddam, and they were terrified of his security apparatus going after them and their families. Roger that; they were also supremely terrified by the prospect of Uday and Qusay coming to power, after Saddam.

Why was the Iraqi Army more afraid of Saddam than us? Because our entire history with Saddam was a history of confrontations and engagements in which we had failed to take Saddam down.

When we'd talk to Iraqi Army soldiers and commanders, even relatively junior guys, they would give us a detailed history lesson on U.S. involvement with Saddam. They'd say, "You Americans gave Saddam assistance during the Iraq-Iran War. You guys made a conscious decision to leave him in power during the Persian Gulf War. And all these bombing campaigns since 1991 . . . You guys show up every few years and you bomb a bunch of stuff, and you talk a lot of trash about Saddam being an evil dictator—and we know he's an evil dictator—but then you leave him in power."

Keep in mind: None of these guys were keen on any geopolitical constructs voiced inside the Beltway, and none of them gave a hoot in hell about realpolitik. They all had firsthand experience in dealing with geopolitics, at a grassroots level, with their lives in the balance. They'd seen history written in blood, not ink.

So, we'd be talking to an Iraqi Army brigade commander about rising up against Saddam and he'd say, "That's great; as soon as I know that Saddam is gone and he is not coming back, then I am with you. But I will be damned if I am going to be the first brigade commander to rise up against him, because based on past experience, what will happen is that the *Mukhabarat* will show up and put a bullet in my head, kill my family, kill all my officers, and the U.S. won't do anything about it. Even if my entire brigade rebels against Saddam, the only thing that will happen is one of Saddam's Republican Guard divisions will appear in force and wipe us off the face of the earth and the United States will not do anything about that, either."

Now, by the time of the ground war, we were taking down *Mukhabarat*.

We wanted to destroy as much of Saddam's secret police as possible.

We understood what Saddam's tools of control were, and our objective was to go after these guys and hunt down the ones who were terrorizing Iraqis into supporting Saddam.

Our primary objective here was, If you are *Mukhabarat*, you've got one of two choices: Either we are going to kill you, or you are going to stop coming to work.

You can fade away, for the time being, but if you keep showing up as *Mukhabarat* in all the places you keep showing up, you are going to die. We sent that message to the *Mukhabarat*.

Our Kurdish *peshmerga* deep recon teams were one big element here.

They were fluent in Arabic and Iraqi dialects of Arabic.

Every time the *Mukhabarat* displaced, our *peshmerga* teams would track them down and hit them again. Also, we were doing that with our existing assets, with our human intelligence network.

On our own, we were striking at *Mukhabarat* and the Special Security Organization with our sabotage teams. Theoretically, the Scorpions were going to carry out the sabotage missions. Finally, in early February 2003, headquarters told us to do what we had been telling them to do since July 2002, which was to train and equip Kurdish *peshmerga* sabotage teams.

As is typical of pretty much everything else in this operation, essentially we had to do this with all of our own resources in Kurdistan and Northern Iraq. Green light on *peshmerga* sabotage teams, so we stood up a sizable program to train them, out of our own personnel—roughly one hundred Kurds, in addition to our deep recon teams.

We taught them fundamentals on demolitions—how to cut fuse cord, how to emplace blasting caps, all the basics—and then worked toward more-advanced concepts. Then, we took them on explosive ranges, building charges and detonating charges.

We moved on to training for specific missions, because different missions require different techniques. If you're taking out a railway line, as opposed to dropping a radio tower, you need different charges and different techniques.

Each mission had to be thoroughly planned, because we were doing our utmost not only to save our Kurdish sabotage teams, but also to save civilian lives. All of the guys who did the training were explosives experts and bomb technicians we had assigned to my team. This was strictly done out of Salahuddin and out of KDP territory—there were no *peshmerga* deep reconnaissance teams or sabotage teams operating out of Qal'ah Chulan.

Bob Woodward gives the impression in *Plan of Attack* that there was a spontaneous bombing of rail lines in Northern Iraq by the Kurds, with some Arab participation. That is not at all true. The Kurds were instrumental in undertaking the sabotage campaign, and the actual teams were Kurdish teams. The entire sabotage campaign up north was created, planned, and orchestrated by my team, in Salahuddin.

There was nothing spontaneous about it, and there was no Arab participation.

Moses, a veteran demolitions specialist, was fundamental to the whole Kurdish sabotage operation against Saddam's regime, up north. Moses was an expert bomb technician and he was at one with the Kurds. Key ground truth here is that we were never staffed by CIA headquarters to run a sabotage campaign. Roger that; we improvised, adapted, and overcame; had we not, it would've put our own lives in greater peril.

Seeing as headquarters had fallen in love with the Scorpions, and because they had refused since July 2002 to accept our continuous proposals to train, man, and arm Kurdish sabotage teams, our base was not staffed or equipped to support a sabotage campaign.

We had to do it on a shoestring.

We had only three trained demolitions specialists, and the Turks had denied us demolitions gear and explosives.

Yes, the Turks had flat-out refused to let us bring in explosives.

And we had long since inspected the explosives stocks of the Kurds, virtually all of which was unusable because they were so old and poorly maintained.

We were forced by the Turks to smuggle in fuse cord, detonators, blasting caps, timers, plastic explosives—everything we needed for the sabotage campaign against Saddam in Northern Iraq.

Was Bush divorced from reality, yet again? Hell yes. Johnny Cash was born in Arkansas, there are big skies in Montana, catfish swim in the Mississippi, and Bush is divorced from reality. It was really crazy.

At the point of the shooting war in February 2003, the entire effort of the U.S. government in Northern Iraq was reduced to a few guys smuggling explosives into Iraq because our NATO ally, Turkey, refused to let us bring them into Iraq.

My team—a handful of guys using virtually nothing and operating on a shoestring, smuggling explosives across the Turkish border—was able to put together a professional sabotage operation in thirty days in February and March 2003, against all odds.

The most notable act—Woodward got it very wrong in *Plan of Attack*—was a Kurdish sabotage team raid against a major rail line that was a vital logistical link to Iraqi Army 5th Corps, which was headquartered in Mosul and commanded Iraqi artillery at Dormeez.

Now, this was the rail link that the Scorpions had been trained to destroy. That was the entire reason for the existence of the four-man Scorpion team, which was all that remained of the Scorpions by early February 2003, when they mutinied, saying: "I want my Mama. I want hot lamb *shawarma* in pita bread, dates, and hot sweet tea; give me some cigarettes. I am not going to help take down Saddam. Good-bye!"

I had a hard time convincing my team not to kill the Scorpions who mutinied. I had guys walking up to me, saying, "Can I go shoot the Scorpions in the head now?" We hated them. We had to babysit them up in the mountains and make sure they were able to feed their addictions to DVD porn and beer. They were just losers.

Our Kurds went in, infiltrated across the Green Line, made their way to a spot twenty miles south of Mosul, and conducted the sabotage raid.

Our Kurdish sabotage team did not just take out the rail line—they took it out at the ideal moment, exactly as we'd planned, which was just prior to a major troop movement by Iraqi Army 5th Corps.

The mission was planned meticulously and executed flawlessly, and because of that, the Kurds took the entire Iraqi Army train down.

In excess of ninety railroad cars were laid on their side—an absolutely perfect raid. This was the first time that a raid like this had been done since World War II—almost sixty years since a U.S. combat operation of that order against a rail line.

Very shortly before this sabotage mission went down, Langley had contacted me and said: "There is concern that when you blow up the rail line, people on the train might get hurt." Unquote, verbatim. Correct; it's like CIA headquarters decided: "Hmmm . . . Now that we're actually going to war in Iraq—what does that mean? How does one fight a war? Will anyone get hurt?"

At this point in the deployment, my sense of humor had evaporated.

I said several things to headquarters, in response. "First of all," I said, "if you blow up a train track and a train rolls over that section of destroyed track, I am pretty sure that somebody is going to get hurt. It is very astute of you to figure that out.

"Second, I'm very confused. Because, as I understand it, you are getting ready to invade this country and blow the living shit out of it, killing thousands of people, so why are you all obsessing about the fact that we are going to wreck one train on the main logistical link to the core force of Saddam's 5th Corps? This is the rail line that feeds the heart of Saddam's forces in the Northern Front of the Iraqi Army. Saddam can't fire artillery shells at Dahuk if he can't get more artillery shells, by train, to the Iraqi Army at Dormeez.

"And just to remind you, headquarters— you selected the target. This was a target for the Scorpions, remember? We just inherited the target. Now we are actually doing what you do in war, which is preparing to kill the enemy, and you are telling me you don't want us to kill the enemy."

They replied, "There may be civilians on the train."

"That's correct," I said. "There may be civilians in downtown Baghdad, too, and you are preparing to blow the living shit out of downtown Baghdad. Are you kidding me? There are also civilians in Dahuk, and if we destroy this rail line, no Iraqi Army artillery shells fired from Dormeez will rain steel on Dahuk."

At some point in this conversation with Iraq Operations Group, they told me to shut up. They then said, "The decision has been made; you have to warn the Iraqi Army that you are going to blow up the rail line."

"Really?" I said. "And what genius has decided we need to warn the Iraqi Army before we blow up the rail line that feeds the Iraqi Army, up north?"

Iraq Operations Group then told me that CIA director George Tenet had made that decision.

He wanted us to warn the Iraqi Army before we made the raid.

At this point, I said, "It's very nice that you all are concerned about people that may or may not be on this train, but my immediate concern is for the safety of my Kurdish sabotage teams who are going to be fifty miles behind enemy lines raiding the Iraqi Army. Now, does it matter to anybody at headquarters that by warning the Iraqi Army about the raid, we are going to get our Kurds killed? Has that crossed anybody's mind at Langley?"

Headquarters' response was, "Shut up. The decision has been made that you will have your sabotage teams fifty miles behind enemy lines. Once the Kurds place the charges, they will call the railroad in Mosul, and before they set off the explosion, they will say, 'We are blowing up your railroad.' That will give the Iraqis time to stop the train."

Exactly. You can just imagine the French Resistance calling one of Hitler's generals in 1944 and warning him that a French sabotage team is going to derail a Nazi train. Roger that; the OSS in Northwestern Thailand never warned the Japanese Army before they raided an enemy packhorse supply train in the mountains during World War II.

So, I said to Iraq Operations Group, "Great. What number do my guys have to call? My guys can speak Arabic, but this is not Amtrak, and there's no customer service number for the Iraqi Army in Mosul."

Iraq Operations Group had no idea what they were talking about. They couldn't tell me who my sabotage team had to call.

The next scene in this theater of the absurd was that I had to tell the Kurds. I had to go talk with chief of KDP intelligence, Masrour Barzani, and tell him this. You can imagine how delighted he was to hear these instructions, which contradicted everything in the history of warfare. Masrour looked at me like I had three heads.

"Are you Americans for real?" he said. I could tell he was thinking, *Ah, the Americans are always talking like they are going to kick ass, but they want to warn Saddam and his Iraqi Army before the Baathists even get out the door. How is it that the Americans have ever won a war?*

Masrour said, "Well, if this is the only way to get the raid done, I'll have our guys call the main railway station in Mosul and tell them, 'Your rail line is about to blow up; you might want to stop your train.'"

The Kurds made the raid and we blew up the rail line and the train. The Kurds told us, "Our guys called, but nobody picked up the phone in the Mosul railway station." Which is what you'd expect in the Near East, especially when every sheep and its shepherd from Egypt to Iran knew that we were going to war in Iraq.

I called headquarters and reported the operation. They did not say: "Amazing! You guys just pulled off the greatest rail sabotage mission since the Second World War!" The only thing they said to me was: "Did they make the phone call?"

"Yes, they made the phone call," I said, "and you're going to find this hard to believe—in a country where everyone knows that every phone call is monitored by Saddam's *Mukhabarat,* and they are about five minutes away from going to war with the United States so people aren't coming to work anymore here, in the first place—but nobody picked up the phone."

The response from the Iraq Operations Group: "Oh, that is so unfortunate; we have to go brief the director."

That was the great railway mission. We got no congratulations from headquarters, none whatsoever. Our demolitions specialists—all of our explosives and ordnance guys who put together that program out of nothing, creating this entire sabotage campaign—deserve the highest credit. It is just incredible what they accomplished. Nobody was lost, nobody detected, nobody captured, nobody killed, nobody wounded, deep behind enemy lines, in an operation we pulled together at the drop of a hat and planned meticulously, after Washington had just spent nearly a year and tens of millions of dollars to create a sabotage operation, the Scorpions, which was an abject failure.

When Tenet wrote his memoirs, he had nothing to say about the Kurdish sabotage teams who carried out extraordinary covert missions up north, not one word. Yet Tenet describes the losers and rapists and felons, the Scorpions, as heroes? That is obscene. Not only do the Scorpions deserve no credit whatsoever, but it's also an insult to all of the Kurds who put it on the line and were heroic and absolutely effective in combat.

It's the Lost Surrender of Mosul that truly haunts us still in Iraq, however, and always will.

Getting 5th Corps Iraqi Army to surrender was one of our core objectives, since March 2002, and necessary to the surrender of Saddam's Northern Front—150,000 Iraqi Army soldiers.

To that end, the Kurds helped us incredibly. We'd already lost Kurdish assets who'd dared to reach out to the Iraqi Army with surrender messages.

Shortly before the Air War started, we arranged with the Kurds to use an existing radio station, in KDP territory in Erbil, and we began a regular series of prerecorded surrender messages, in English and Arabic. We used English deliberately, even though we knew that only a small number of people would understand, to ensure that there was no ambiguity about Americans being in the area.

Sheryl Crow's "A Change Would Do You Good," Toby Keith's "The Angry American," and Joe Diffie's "Prop Me Up against the Jukebox When I Die," were also on the tape, with a lot of Rolling Stones, too. The surrender messages were direct and clear: "Don't die for Saddam. You guys want what we want—an end to the nightmare of Saddam. We don't have a quarrel with anybody but Saddam." In that context, just to add a little edge to it, we took this small transmitter, about the size of a steamer trunk, and loaded it with a ton of prerecorded surrender messages and music. We hooked it up to the power in an old sedan, so it could run directly off the juice.

Kurdish agents drove it into Mosul and parked it a half-mile from 5th Corps headquarters. Kurdish agents reported back to us that the surrender messages ran until that car ran out of gas. "Lowrider" rocked on it, too. The whole point was to make the Iraqi Army feel completely impotent.

Another key element of the surrender mission was tons of surrender pamphlets, all in Arabic. Translated, they read, "We are not here to harm you; we are here to take down Saddam." The Kurds handed these out in markets, outside mosques and churches, and the streets in Mosul were just littered with these surrender messages in mid-March 2003.

In early March, as we'd been initiating the surrender propaganda, we received cardboard boxes from Langley. They were filled with all sizes of a flag I'd never seen before, and decals. There was no documentation or message traffic about the flags. We actually thought that maybe somebody screwed up at headquarters and these were supposed to go to some embassy in South America.

We contacted headquarters and they told us, "This is the new Iraqi flag. We designed it." Some guys in a room at Langley had literally drawn up this flag. We showed it to the Kurds, and Sarwar, our main contact, said, "This looks like the flag of some African country." He was just very, very puzzled. It was another Through-the-Looking-Glass moment, where we decided, "This is just too ridiculous. We are not handing these over to the Iraqis, the Kurds, or anyone else. We will lose all credibility." We took all of those flags and dumped them in burn barrels and lit them up.

Several weeks later, when the war was on in earnest, headquarters sent us message traffic, telling us how to pass out the flags "among the population, as you cross the Green Line." I told headquarters directly, "We cannot distribute the flags because I destroyed them all. The reaction here is that they are just too ridiculous, and the bogus flags will destroy our credibility."

Headquarters got really pissed off. I am absolutely sure that they'd taken the CIA-created flags of liberated Iraq to the White House and Bush was waiting to see their cocked-up flag being waved in the streets.

That flag was devoid of any symbolism that had anything to do with Iraq. Meanwhile, I was thinking, "You haven't been able to give me 90 percent of anything I've needed, but you are so damn happy to waste my operational time with this stupid project."

And the guys on the team were disgusted. It was just another example of how out-of-touch Washington was with the reality on the ground in Iraq.

The 173rd Airborne dropped at Hareer Airfield on March 26, 2003. Right after they dropped, we started getting hit with Iraqi Army surface-to-surface missile.

The Iraqi Army 5th Corps was firing the missiles at the 173rd, at Hareer airfield, and at Salahuddin. The 5th Corps always fired at night. That continued every night, for a week. Sometimes one missile a night, and sometimes several. Their aim tended to vary widely. The missiles frequently landed in a hillside. I reckon that a missile crew had been ordered to launch, but in some cases they didn't spend a whole lot of time aiming. On one night, we had four surface-to-surface missiles hit near Salahuddin, including one that hit 200 meters from our base house.

Working with 10th Group, we discovered that 5th Corps had a spy in Salahuddin, a forward observer. We hunted him down, narrowed down his location, and identified a particular section of Salahuddin he was broadcasting from. He went off the air and disappeared. Even after all the *Mukhabarat* and Iraqi Army we'd taken off the street in Salahuddin, we realized that there were still a few of Saddam's spies out there.

We were reporting all this to Washington, all the details on us getting attacked, and we got no commentary back at all, other than more questions about the flags.

Washington stayed pissed off about the flags and did not care about us nearly getting killed.

Roger that; we were under fire from 5th Corps Iraqi Army and it meant nothing to Washington. Except to one guy in a cubicle at Langley.

Whenever there was a surface-to-surface missile launch, about five minutes after impact, some guy in Washington would call, all frantic, to tell us that they had detected a launch on imagery and wanting to give us a heads up. We would tell him thanks for the timely info and remind him, every time, that the missile had already struck. He was just some guy sitting in a cubicle somewhere watching a screen and the only guy paying attention, I guess.

Each morning after the missile attacks, we'd collect the scraps. Just one of those missiles would've killed everyone in the compound, all of us. Those were big surface-to-surface missiles, roughly the same size as SCUD missiles. And Washington never responded to our messages about getting hit with missiles. They apparently had more important things to worry about.

When the paratroopers dropped, it was surreal. The 173rd dropped in at Hareer airfield, which was in Kurdish hands, and had been for years.

We drove down to the airstrip on March 27th in a couple of Land Cruisers. We rolled up and I was in the lead vehicle.

Now, we were warm and dry with the Rolling Stones and Sheryl Crow pumping out of our Land Cruisers, drinking coffee as we approached the guards.

The paratroopers had a couple of machine guns set up at checkpoints. It wasn't raining at the time, even though it had been raining for days and days.

That airfield sits down in a low valley, and when they hit the ground, they must have gone up to their knees in mud. They were just covered in it, soaking wet and miserable. They were standing there at the checkpoint when we rolled up with the tunes rocking, drinking coffee.

"Who are you guys?" a sergeant asked.

"We're your friendly neighborhood CIA," I said, "and we thought we'd welcome you to the neighborhood."

He shrugged and said, "Okay."

I asked him, "Where's your commanding officer?" He pointed vaguely and said, "I think that the CP [command post] is down by the airstrip." He didn't know where his commanding officer was, and he didn't know exactly where the CP was, either. Fortunately, he let us go ahead.

Driving down to the airfield, we looked at each other and said, "We just drove through an official U.S. Army checkpoint in a war zone and showed no ID whatsoever." On the one hand, we were happy that they had let us through. On the other hand, we felt that those guards didn't really know where they were.

We drove down to the airstrip, looking for Colonel Mayfield. We eventually found the command post, but he was out on the perimeter. We talked to his staff. They had no instructions to lash up with us. No one had told the 173rd that we were in Iraq. And we had all the field intelligence in the world on Kurdistan and Northern Iraq.

We talked to their intelligence officer, a major. He started asking us random logistical questions, really small stuff. Like, where he could get Mo-gas for their vehicles. I told him that there was a village about a mile from the airfield, with shops and gas stations.

He started pulling out maps. The whole time, now, I was thinking, "How could you have jumped onto this airfield and not known the surrounding villages?"

One of the other staff guys started asking us questions about the bridges on roads over small streams near the airfield, like, "What load will the bridges bear?" These are basic route reconnaissance questions.

I remember looking at him and saying, "We've had 10th Group commandos carrying out extensive field intelligence for us, for over six months. And they've gone over every bridge in Kurdistan. They've certainly done that one, at least three times. Our 10th Group Special Forces commandos sent all those reports to CENTCOM, on official military channels. Haven't you seen any of 10th Group's reports?"

He responded, "I have seen none of that. I have seen nothing from the field here. CENTCOM sent us nothing. All we have are these maps."

He was completely unaware, like the rest of the 173rd, of our presence, the pilot team's presence, 10th Group's presence, and the massive amount of field reporting done by U.S. Army Special Forces.

It was a friggin' crime that in a war zone, where our pilot teams had done a full report on every bridge in Kurdistan—bridge material, tensile strength, dimensions of the support and structural members, loads the bridge will bear, etc.—not one piece of that field intelligence had reached the 173rd.

All the 10th Group commandos on our pilot team from Special Forces had done this incredible reconnaissance, but because none of those reports had gone from CENTCOM to the 173rd, now the 173rd was at war in Iraq and reduced to asking me, Johnny-on-the-spot, "Hey, how much do you think that bridge will bear?"

After this, we maintained regular, daily contact with the 173rd for a week. We brought some of their intelligence officers and NCOs up to Salahuddin, showed them our setup, and they were also communicating with 10th Group Special Forces, at that point.

Now, very strangely, after a week of solid communications with the 173rd, including direct, face-to-face communications with their commanding officer, Colonel Mayfield, one of our 10th Group commandos told me, "We are no longer allowed to communicate with the 173rd. We should only be communicating with the task force, and our point of contact with the task force is Lieutenant Colonel Robert Waltemeyer, 2nd Battalion Commander, 10th Group Special Forces."

We could not speak or directly communicate in any way with the 173rd at that point, and that was very unfortunate. That was Waltemeyer's decision. My experience, throughout this time, was that we were constantly in a mode of reaching out to the U.S. military and everyone else, saying, "What can we do to help you?" But the only people who rejected our help were U.S. military, especially Waltemeyer.

A lot of that has to do with personalities. Certainly, many people we dealt with in the U.S. military got along with us superbly and were very courteous and professional, with everyone on our teams.

But a few select individuals, like Waltemeyer, were not.

In my opinion, for Waltemeyer, the idea that the war in Northern Iraq would end with the CIA accepting the surrender of the main force, the Iraqi Army, was a nightmare.

His attitude toward us, from the day he landed, was manifest. The 10th Group commandos on my team had it the worst. They were thinking the whole time, "I've got to go back to 10th Group when this is all over, and Waltemeyer hates me and hates my guys, for having been 10th Group Special Forces attached to the CIA."

And Waltemeyer's ego, his refusal to listen to me and anyone else on my team, I think had a lot to do with the greatest tragedy of March to May, 2003—the Lost Surrender of Mosul.

It was an incredible opportunity to get a formal surrender from the entire 5th Corps of the Iraqi Army, 50,000 soldiers and their commanders, the mayor of Mosul, and all of Saddam's government up north.

It would have damn likely led to a formal surrender from the Iraqi Army, in the entire country.

Again, the Kurds did all they could to help us gain that surrender, but a main goal since March 2002—getting the Northern Front of the Iraqi Army to surrender—was pissed away by Lieutenant Colonel Robert Waltemeyer, a battalion commander in 10th Group Special Forces.

The key truth here is that it was absolutely bedrock in our strategy for the U.S. to co-opt the Iraqi Army, 150,000 soldiers, on the Northern Front; that had been a central goal of the U.S. government since March 2002.

Come April 11, 2003, my counterterrorist team leader in Dahuk and General Babakir Zebari, who commanded 27,000 Kurdish *peshmerga* in northern Kurdistan, had convinced the Iraqi Army 5th Corps Commander, the mayor of Mosul, key tribal sheikhs, and former senior Baathists to offer the keys to the city to the United States and the Coalition.

General Babakir Zebari and my counterterrorist team leader in Dahuk set up the meeting, south of Dahuk, right on the Green Line between Kurdish and Iraqi forces. With the meeting arranged and the surrender verbally agreed on, Zebari told Waltemeyer, "You need to come on down and take the surrender."

We, in conjunction with the KDP, were in contact with a whole group of Iraqi Army, including the 5th Group commander and the mayor of Mosul, and they offered to surrender the city and the entire 5th Corps to the United States.

That's 50,000 Iraqi Army soldiers, all their command, all their weapons, all their supplies, all their tanks, artillery, mechanized infantry, all their vehicles and all their gear, their headquarters base, and all their fire bases.

Now, the entire Iraqi Army in Northern Iraq was 150,000.

Roger that; had we gained the surrender of 5th Corps, the core of the Iraqi Army's Northern Front, we knew it could have led directly to the surrender of the entire Northern Front of the Iraqi Army.

We were aiming for formal surrender from all of the Iraqi Army, and while we knew it would be difficult, formal surrender from 5th Corps would have been the first jewel in that crown.

The ultimate crown jewel that everyone had been seeking for fourteen months was now right in our lap. In addition, Dormeez would have been removed completely as a Baathist dagger aimed at Dahuk, and of course, there would have been no looting in Mosul and Northern Iraq.

With the surrender of Iraqi Army 5th Corps, we would have rolled in, taken over 5th Corps HQ, and taken over the running of Mosul.

The catch is that Washington had informed us back in February and March 2003, that we, the CIA, were forbidden to accept the surrender of any Iraqi Army units. This was Rumsfeld's decision.

Rumsfeld would not allow the CIA to accept the surrender or take control of any Iraqi Army units; only the Department of Defense could handle these tasks.

Rumsfeld didn't like our role in Iraq. He was still pissed off about the CIA in Afghanistan.

Rumsfeld felt that the Agency had made his guys look bad in Afghanistan because we got on the ground first, got more done, and the real campaign was largely an Agency-fought operation, lashed up with some U.S. Army Special Forces.

No way in hell would Rumsfeld want the Iraq War to make him look like he was playing second fiddle to the Agency once again.

There's no way, with that mind-set, that Rumsfeld would allow us to accept surrender and take control of Iraqi Army units—which was tragic, as events in Mosul proved.

Zebari had received an offer of surrender from 5th Corps Iraqi Army, an open door to the ultimate crown jewel, leading to surrender of all Iraqi Army soldiers in the entire country.

This was in Mosul on April 11, 2003, two days after Saddam's statue was toppled in Baghdad while the then-nascent Iraqi insurgency was firing heavy machine guns and mortars, RPGs, and small arms at U.S. and Coalition forces in Iraq.

But to get the surrender of Mosul from verbal to formal, signed, and for real surrender, we had to go to Lieutenant Colonel Robert Waltemeyer, who seemed to hate us.

This was like going to Satan and asking him to shake hands with Saint Michael the Archangel; that train is not going to leave the station.

How much did Waltemeyer hate us and despise the CIA? In Salahuddin and Dahuk, we had Whiskey, a U.S. Air Force air combat controller, on our Salahuddin team and our Dahuk team, calling in air strikes. Whiskey was a quiet, bearded guy, very sharp, and blended in perfectly on this clandestine operation. He was the ideal guy for these missions. Whiskey was, in many ways, the most valuable guy we had in Dahuk.

Waltemeyer found out in the middle of March 2003 that we had a USAF air combat controller who was calling in air strikes on Iraqi targets. Waltemeyer had Whiskey's clearance to call air strikes removed: Whiskey's call sign, his authentication, and everything he needed to be able to do his duty at war—officially removed.

Waltemeyer pulled Whiskey's clearances because he did not want us, the CIA and our joint team, engaging Iraqi targets in Northern Iraq. He did not want our help, period. Waltemeyer would have been happy if we had left the area of operations, entirely.

Waltemeyer did not tell Whiskey or anyone else on our team that he had done this. And remember, we had 10th Group Special Forces attached to us, in Salahuddin, Dahuk, and Qal'ah Chulan.

Forty-eight hours after Waltemeyer removed Whiskey's status as a combat air controller, Whiskey was up on the Green Line with our Dahuk counterterrorists and they were in a tight spot, about to be overrun by a regiment of 5th Corps Iraqi Army. Whiskey started talking to USAF B-52s in the area, asking them to strike at the Iraqi Army and save him and our Dahuk counterterrorists. The B-52s told him, "No, you're not in our system. We can't authenticate your call for fire. We cannot engage."

Roger that; the United States Air Force had been denied the mission to save Whiskey, a USAF air combat controller, and all of our CIA assets with him, because of Waltemeyer's order. Not only did Waltemeyer get Whiskey's status removed, but he also came on the net in the middle of the call for fire and made sure the air strike was not sent. Whiskey and our guys had to run like hell; they barely got out of there without being killed. It was effectively a death sentence on Whiskey and our CIA officers that accompanied him.

Upon returning to Dahuk, Whiskey immediately inquired through official channels why he no longer had authority to call in air strikes. The U.S. Air Force told him, "Lieutenant Colonel Robert Waltemeyer, 10th Group Special Forces, United States Army, removed you from the system. You cannot call in air strikes."

Later, behind Waltemeyer's back, 10th Group commandos got other people's call signs for Whiskey, so that the Dahuk team could still call in air strikes. This was all 10th Group; and thank God their commandos helped each other.

It wasn't just Whiskey; Waltemeyer also turned off Lightning and Samson's authorization to call in air strikes. They were Special Operations commandos with full authorization to call in air strikes, but after Waltemeyer, they also had to use other people's call signs to call in air strikes on Iraqi units.

That tells you where Waltemeyer was coming from. Waltemeyer was the battalion commander for that sector of Northern Iraq. From the second he arrived in-country, he made it crystal clear that he did not want to work with us.

It is unconscionable to take an action like that against Americans in a war zone—Americans who are part of a mission with other Americans to strike and kill our enemies in the field.

Lightning and Samson were instrumental to our success in the field. They were highly experienced and extremely effective Special Operations commandos with full authority to call in air strikes. Simply because Waltemeyer did not want to work with the CIA, Lightning's and Samson's lives, and the lives of all who were with them on missions against the Iraqi Army, were seriously endangered.

Now, in the wake of Waltemeyer's actions under-mining our men, my Dahuk counterterrorist team leader had to go and tell Waltemeyer that we had the golden opportunity to accept the formal surren-der of Mosul on April 11, 2003.

Waltemeyer showed up late at the meeting in a belligerent mood, with an entire set of horrifically bureaucratic conditions, which he then subjected the Iraqis to—a colossal mistake for which we paid, dearly. Waltemeyer hadn't told anyone on our side that he would be issuing these demands to the Iraqis. He completely blindsided us, and General Zebari, with his list of demands—a long list of bureaucratic terms of surrender which he demanded that the 5th Corps commander and the mayor of Mosul sign off on before any formal surrender could go down. It was a real insult to the Iraqis, from a Near Eastern and an Arab standpoint. And we were in the Near East, dealing with Arabs.

The proper way to do this in the Near East is to show up, drink tea, stroke these guys, let them deliver whatever speeches they wanted to deliver, and then basically say, "Thank you very much. We are grateful to accept your surrender, and we'll work out the details later." Then, you sit on the side with their aides and review the details of the surrender and get the signatures you need. With Arabs, and, generally speaking, with anyone in the Near East, that's how you get it done.

We would never have subjected them to the humiliating experience of losing face before the first cup of tea was served.

Yet Waltemeyer did not seem to understand that in Asia and the Near East saving face is a paramount element of negotiation.

So, the meeting broke down immediately. The Iraqis were incensed at Waltemeyer—well and truly pissed off. They went from happy to surrender to us, to very unhappy to be in our presence, at the drop of a hat. Waltemeyer had no appreciation of the ground he was standing on.

River, the 2nd Battalion 10th Group Special Forces operations sergeant major, was outside the meeting when Waltemeyer was busy "losing the surrender of the main force, Northern Front, Iraqi Army," as River said to me on December 9, 2007, confirming the Dahuk counterterrorist team leader's firsthand account of the meeting.

River also confirmed the counterterrorists' firsthand account of Waltemeyer removing Whiskey, Lightning, and Samson's authorizations to call in air strikes, and Waltemeyer's "order to send that *peshmerga* across the Green Line to parlay with the Iraqi Army—everyone in 10th Group was aware of that, it was unprofessional and grossly incompetent of Waltemeyer. His actions got that *peshmerga* killed on the Green Line, and in Mosul, he lost that surrender," said River.

Sam continued his account of what happened next:

The Iraqi Army fell away but did not go away, from that point on. No doubt they manned the ranks of the insurgency, and it never had to go down like that, at all.

The surrender train had left the station, and the peace train had left the station: Waltemeyer derailed both of them.

The entire Northern Front of the Iraqi Army had tried to surrender—they wanted to surrender—and they had verbally communicated that decision, but Waltemeyer lost that opportunity to end the war and win the peace.

The Northern Front of the Iraqi Army, 150,000 Iraqi Army soldiers, disappeared their uniforms, kept their Kalashnikovs and RPGs, and never surrendered, from that point forward. As did the rest of the Iraqi Army, for that matter. The Lost Surrender of Mosul ensured that the surrender of the entire Iraqi Army would be lost, which indeed it was. For us CIA counterterrorist officers in Iraq, it was the most horrifying experience we could imagine: The main American focus in Northern Iraq had been to find a way to get 5th Corps to surrender, true since March 2002. We had delivered that surrender to Waltemeyer on a silver platter. If the surrender had taken place, we would have controlled Mosul, operating out of 5th Corps HQ, with 50,000 Iraqis working for us—the entire governmental structure in Mosul, in the heart of Northern Iraq.

At that point, we could have pointed to the rest of Iraq and said, "Just lash up with the Americans, lay down your arms. Saddam is not coming back. Look at what happened in Mosul!" That was one of the main reasons we had been bore-sighted on getting the 5th Corps Iraqi Army to surrender since March 2002.

That was why we wanted to get the Northern Front to surrender.

That was precisely the point, the reason why our main thrust, in terms of our mission to take down Saddam, had been to get the 5th Corps Iraqi Army, the heart of Saddam's Northern Front, to surrender.

All of those Sunnis, terrified of what was going to happen to them in a post-Sunni-dominated Iraq, would have been able to point to the example of Mosul's smooth transition, rather than the chaos and anarchy that arose without the surrender. Where was Bush on all this? Asleep at the wheel. Bush reacted to Waltemeyer's decision with complete detachment even though Waltemeyer had blown his chance to achieve a massive strategic victory in Mosul.

We went from mid-April 2003, when we were on the verge of walking into Mosul and literally being handed the keys to the city, to six weeks later, when Bremer made his decision to disband the Iraqi Army. Bush had now managed to create a situation in Iraq where we were hunkered down and surrounded by hostile forces on all sides, and completely powerless to control the chaos.

The Kurds, looking at U.S. decisions in Iraq, thought the Bush administration was manned with complete idiots. The Kurds said to us, "How can the U.S. military walk away from the surrender of 150,000 Iraqi Army soldiers in Northern Iraq? Why does Bush do that? Why does Bush refuse the keys to the city of Mosul? You are your own worst enemy." The Kurds were more puzzled and confounded than ever by Bush, after the Lost Surrender of Mosul.

Just look at Mosul, a city of half a million people, one of the three main cities in Iraq, along with Basra and Baghdad. And you're going to destroy the entire government and security apparatus, in a city of half a million. You're going to walk away from the entire surrender of the entire city. But that is exactly what happened, and the administration never batted an eye.

So, if you won't accept the surrender of the largest Iraqi Army unit in Northern Iraq, and you won't let the Kurds enter Mosul, and you have only a handful of U.S. troops on the ground, exactly what force on the ground in Mosul is going to control the situation? And the answer, of course, is: *There isn't one.* Was that really such a difficult concept to understand?

When Bremer made the decision to disband the Iraqi Army, what was in his head—I don't need an army? How did he plan on controlling an entire nation without the Iraqi Army? And there was nobody in the White House, nobody in the U.S. government, who said, "Hey, buddy, you might want to think about this." Thousands of Americans have died because of that decision. Many thousands of Iraqis have died, and millions have fled as refugees to Jordan and other Arab nations.

Could we have won the war, and truly *ended* the war, in May 2003?

Yes, but I was convinced, on the ground in Iraq in mid-April, that we could've ended the war in April 2003.

The Lost Surrender of Mosul, looking back, was the most grievous but by no means the last massive lost opportunity by Bush to end the war and win the peace.

Why did Bush fail? When your modus operandi is to be divorced from reality, that includes being asleep at the wheel when it comes to the reality of war. The Lost Surrender of Mosul is a direct consequence of Bush's incompetent leadership—Bush's failure of command.

In Mosul on April 11, 2003, meanwhile, even after Waltemeyer's blunder, my Dahuk counterterrorist team leader and Zebari convinced the 5th Corps commander, the mayor of Mosul, and the key tribal sheikhs in Northern Iraq, that all was not lost, saying: "We're going to reconvene in a few hours, carry on, and meet tomorrow to get the formal surrender done."

We all agreed to break for a few hours and get organized so that we could reconvene in a forum where we could get some real work done, repairing the bridge that Waltemeyer had nearly burned down. There was still a chance for the formal surrender of 5th Corps Iraqi Army, absolutely.

Waltemeyer went away with his own contingent from 10th Group. Zebari rolled back to Dahuk.

My Dahuk team leader was with him, along with three 10th Group commandos. They had field radios with 10th Group frequencies, which they listened to all the time. What they heard, riding back to Dahuk, was Waltemeyer issuing orders to 10th Group A teams to enter Mosul—right at that moment. Roger that; Waltemeyer had to know that if he did this, it would subvert the formal surrender of Mosul. And he went ahead and did it anyway.

On Pearl Harbor Day, 2007, a 10th Group Special Force commando confirmed that he had heard Waltemeyer order 10th Group Special Forces into Mosul twenty minutes after the meeting to ensure that the surrender of Mosul had broken up. He also confirmed Sam's account of Waltemeyer's rude, belligerent, and insulting behavior toward the tribal chiefs and Iraqis gathered in Mosul on April 11, 2003.

"My Dahuk team leader and Zebari had just left Waltemeyer in Mosul," Sam said, sipping Kentucky bourbon, continuing his account:

It hadn't been twenty minutes since they had talked face-to-face with Waltemeyer, and they were all in agreement about getting the surrender of Mosul done. Waltemeyer had not mentioned a goddamn thing to them, or anyone else, about entering Mosul.

Twenty minutes later, Waltemeyer unilaterally ordered the U.S. Army into Mosul, ignoring not only the CIA, but also the commanding officer of the entire sector of Northern Kurdistan, General Babakir Zebari, who had over one thousand Kurdish *peshmerga* inside Mosul.

Like Zebari, we were completely astounded. As my Dahuk team leader said to me that day, "We were just talking to this guy twenty minutes ago, and we were right on the verge of getting 150,000 Iraqi Army soldiers here to surrender, ending the threat from the Iraqi Army in all of Northern Iraq. And now Waltemeyer has decided to throw that opportunity away and roll into Mosul."

The Dahuk counterterrorists turned around and went into Mosul on April 11, 2003. From a real shot at surrender and a fast track to peace, we marched headlong into anarchy. The Dahuk team also took five hundred KDP *peshmerga,* armed with Kalashnikovs, RPGs, and machine guns.

We had a dedicated battalion of Kurdish *peshmerga* working directly for us, under Dahuk team leader command. They set up at the former base in Mosul, the Adnan division of the Republican Guard. There was already a lot of chaos and looting in Mosul, and shooting in the streets. A lot of madness. Dahuk counterterrorists and the *peshmerga* began taking machine-gun fire, sniper fire, and just getting a lot of incoming at that base.

After a couple days, they relocated, moving to a large villa on the Tigris River that had belonged to one of Saddam's brothers-in-law. There wasn't a specific organized resistance, but already in Mosul, a lot of low-level attacks and a number of KDP *peshmerga* under our command got killed.

There were almost no Americans in the city. The biggest group that came in was the 26th Marine Expeditionary Unit, U.S. Marine Corps. We went from a situation where we could have had the entire 5th

Corps, the police force, and everything else, under
our command, to utter chaos, mayhem, havoc, and
anarchy. The Marines began taking heavy fire at the
airfield.

With the formal surrender of Mosul, American counterterrorists and clandestine field officers under Sam's command
would have held the keys to the city on April 11, 2003.

These were men fluent in the languages, culture, and terrain of the Near East, and ideally suited to gain victory, end
the war, and win the peace.

The U.S. military on the ground in Northern Iraq and
Kurdistan—other than one lieutenant colonel in the U.S. Army,
Waltemeyer—had excellent relations with the CIA, solid rap-
port and respect, and lashed up in Sam's team in Salahuddin.

All counterterrorist teams in Iraq were war fighters and
field intelligence specialists from every arm of the U.S. Special Operations community, along with the best clandestine
assets in the American government, in the Near East.

Together, from July 2002 to April 2003, they had carried
out innumerable counterterrorist missions in Iraq, and were
responsible for determining that Al-Qaeda had built a chemical and biological weapons center near the Iranian border.

They had eliminated Saddam's secret police, the *Mukhabarat,* as a threat in Northern Iraq.

They had built and maintained deep bridges of rapport
and understanding with the Kurds, and engineered the foundation for a formal surrender of Mosul.

They had excellent rapport and relationships with 10th
Group commander, Colonel Charlie Cleveland; with Lieutenant

Colonel Tovo, 3rd BN 10th Group commander; with Major General Osman, USMC; with Massoud Barzani, Jalal Talabani, leader of the Patriotic Union of Kurdistan and later, President of Iraq, General Babakir Zebari, and General Mustafa Amin; and with the entire Kurdish political and military leadership of both the KDP and the PUK, including their intelligence services.

The American counterterrorists and clandestine field officers had also built significant bridges to the Shia leadership in the south, and those lines of communication were wide open, the traffic was two-way, and so was the respect.

They were the only Americans in Iraq with rock-solid relationships with major power brokers from the two ethnic groups—the Shia and the Kurds—which together make up 80 percent of Iraq.

Sam's teams would have been able to tell the mayor of Mosul and the Iraqi Army up north what to do. The Coalition, however, went from the surrender train back to the war train. And bottom line, Rumsfeld and Bush are accountable for the Lost Surrender of Mosul, due directly to Rumsfeld's decision in 2002 that only U.S. military could accept Iraqi Army surrenders—a decision Bush never challenged.

As happened so often in his presidency, Bush was once again asleep at the wheel when Rumsfeld raised a sword against the CIA in 2002, which had devastating consequences for a Coalition victory in the Iraq War.

Bush's decision to let stand Rumsfeld's Machiavellian move to keep the CIA out of the operational loop, regarding the surrender of Iraqi forces, denied America and the Coalition a core mission of the Iraq War (the surrender of 5th Corps Iraqi Army), and steered the United States away from victory in Iraq two days after Saddam's statue had fallen in Baghdad on April 9, 2003.

Rumsfeld's decision to eliminate the CIA, structurally, from accepting surrender in Iraq opened the door to failure at war, which is exactly what the United States and the Coalition got in Iraq—be careful what you wish for. Sam not only held Rumsfeld accountable for the Lost Surrender of Mosul, but he also said, "Bush is accountable, as this happened on his watch. He was commander in chief." Sam went on:

Bush led us to war in Iraq but could not lead us to victory and win the peace. Rumsfeld may have been Secretary of Defense, with significant influence, but Bush was in the big chair. Bush was president and commander in chief. Keep in mind that there was no official surrender anywhere else in Iraq at this time, in mid-April 2003.

Waltemeyer was not only the sole Special Forces commander in Iraq who despised us; he was also the only Special Forces of any rank who refused to listen to us, and who was always belligerent toward us.

What Waltemeyer did had tragic consequences for the United States and Coalition forces in Iraq, and with god-awful consequences for the people of Iraq—and moreover, for the Kurds and Shia and Sunni.

This was all in direct contrast to Lieutenant Colonel Tovo and Colonel Cleveland, who listened closely to us, respected us, treated us with dignity and professionalism, and never tried to fuck us over. Thanks to Tovo and Cleveland, we did finally strike at Ansar al-Islam in March 2003, but we did not strike and kill one thousand Islamist terrorists, as the core leadership of Ansar al-Islam had fled since August 2002, and we did not kill anywhere near two hundred Al-Qaeda. That was Bush's failure, and in no way is 10th Group Special Forces responsible for Bush's failure of command in 2002.

On April 14, 2003, the third day after 10th Group entered Mosul, I went down to meet up with my Dahuk team leader and General Zebari and take stock of the situation in Mosul. I took a half-dozen guys, a couple jeeps, and linked up with my Dahuk team leader in a villa on the Tigris River in Mosul. We entered in daylight, passing a lot of abandoned tanks on the way to Mosul.

Driving into Mosul, I reckoned that back at the White House, somebody had marked Mosul with a pushpin on a map of Iraq, and no doubt the White House was saying on April 14th, "We have captured Mosul, and we are now in control of Mosul."

Driving into Mosul three days after the Lost Surrender, there was chaos everywhere. People were stealing everything. It was a continuous low-level riot.

There was no sign of any military or security force of any kind, from any country.

The first U.S. military I saw was a group of about twenty paratroopers—they must have been 173rd—guarding a sandbagged checkpoint position on Freedom Bridge, over the Tigris River.

The checkpoint was in the middle of the bridge, and there wasn't even a platoon of them.

They had M4s and SAWs, and appeared to be attempting to check people going across the bridge. We were listening to "Gimme Shelter" as we drove up. When we rolled down the window and talked to them, they looked at us like we were from Mars.

You're an American soldier at war in Iraq and a couple Land Cruisers pull up, loaded with bearded guys carrying sidearms and submachine guns, smoking cigars, listening to the Rolling Stones, *khaffiyahs* around their necks, and these cats say, "Greetings, my fellow Americans." I remember the senior guy present was a staff sergeant. They had no translator, and they had no Kurds with them. This staff sergeant started talking with me, just desperate for someone to tell him what was going on. He started asking me questions like, "So where's the Republican Guard? What Iraqi units are still in the city?" Like he was expecting a counterattack from the Iraqi military.

I looked at him, thinking, *How do I tell this guy that our own U.S. military engineered the Lost Surrender of Mosul?* Hit me like a landslide.

Oh man, how do you tell him, as a former U.S. Army commander, which is who I am, how do you tell him, a U.S. Army soldier with his life on the line for our country, how do you tell him that?

And I thought, at the same time, *this guy doesn't even have a clue.* I do not mean that disparagingly, at all, I just mean that it was clear that he and his men were getting no information on the ground in Mosul.

I told him, "All the Republican Guard went home, buddy."

He said, "Oh, that's really good, that's great news."

And I said, "I don't know about that, because they also took all their weapons with them when they went home."

I remember thinking, as we drove away, *"This poor guy, for the love of God, somebody has stuck him here in the middle of this bridge in Mosul with twenty guys and they don't have a translator and they don't have* peshmerga *and they don't even really know where they are."*

I was thinking, at that moment, that somebody in Washington is saying, "We have secured all key infrastructure in Mosul," because somebody in Iraq was telling them, "Yes, we have units on the bridges and key road junctions, etc."

But this staff sergeant's capacity with that checkpoint to actually control anything on the ground was absolutely nil.

A few insurgents with RPGs would have destroyed that checkpoint in seconds, of course.

So we went back to our Dahuk team, on the Tigris River. They'd set up there, because even in the midst of the looting, nobody had looted the former palace of Saddam's brother-in-law. All other houses had been looted.

The night before, some of our Kurds had been ambushed in an Arab neighborhood. One of our medics saved some of them. They were already

159

taking fire on the base, also. We set up machine guns on the roof. The only reason that we were surviving was that we had five hundred Kurds guarding us.

We focused immediately on hunting down high-value targets, including Saddam and Chemical Ali. We were also trying to identify sites of significance in Mosul, especially trying to answer the question: "Are there WMD in Mosul, or not?" There were a lot of Saddam's armories and scientific institutions in Mosul which we'd been collecting on for years, and now we could inspect them, on-site.

For instance, the Al Kindi Research Complex, which was a big scientific institute in the heart of Mosul.

Saddam created the Al Kindi Research Complex to develop and research electronics, optic systems, guidance systems, unmanned aerial vehicles (UAVs, like the American Predator system), chemical weapons, and so on.

Because the Iraqis were so concerned about us bombing the Al Kindi Research Complex, they had taken everything of value outside and piled it all up at intervals, very methodically, so that one bomb would not be able to destroy more than one pile of electronics, aeronautical gear, chemical barrels, and optical systems.

We had all sorts of reporting going on, all the time, with people claiming that there was significant nuclear research going on at the Al Kindi Research Complex. It was one of the things that we could not resolve prior to going into Mosul. Now, we could check it out for ourselves.

The Dahuk team discovered, for instance, very sophisticated, computer-operated lathes, which is exactly what you need in order to produce nuclear weapons, and many other sophisticated advanced weapons. These were sitting on pallets in the middle of a quad, like a quad on any college campus. Seventy-five feet away were stacks of barrels, over fifty drums. Likewise, seventy-five feet away from the barrels, there were stacks and stacks of filing cabinets.

My Dahuk team leader was there with three guys and some Kurds, and he told me, "It's going to take a lot of people a lot of time to determine what is here." Keep in mind that there were armed looters rampaging through the halls of the Al Kindi Research Complex at the very same time he was talking to me. My team leader talked with the senior U.S. military commander in Mosul, the Marine commander, and told him that if we didn't secure this place, we'd never figure out what was there.

"I don't have anybody to spare to secure the Al Kindi Research Complex," he told us, and with a force so small, it was understandable. He had to keep the airfield secure and protect his men, at all costs, and he only had a little over two thousand men. So my Dahuk team leader took matters into his own hands and detailed fifty *peshmerga* to secure the Al Kindi Research Complex.

On the west side of the river was Nineveh Woods, and I'd heard from many Iraqi sources, Arabs and Kurds: "I know that Saddam is hiding antiaircraft weapons—" and before they could finish the sentence, I'd say, "Let me guess—Nineveh Woods, right?" It was like a bad running joke with the team: "Elvis is alive and well in Nineveh Woods, and the Ghost of Jimmy Hoffa roams Nineveh Woods every full moon."

So, we went into Nineveh Woods on April 14, 2003. It was amazing, because everything really was there, just as our sources had been telling us.

There really were surface-to-surface missile systems with the rockets sitting right under the trees.

Tanker trucks, and lots of huge tanks for holding chemicals and fuel, partially buried and camouflaged, all spread out at least seventy-five meters apart, with the same principle used at the Al Kindi Research Complex, so that one bomb could not destroy more than one target.

Antiaircraft weapons, wheeled and tracked, all Eastern bloc. We had tanks, surface-to-surface missiles, radar systems, high-value enemy weapons everywhere. Nobody was guarding any of this. The Iraqi Army had disappeared.

We drove up a road and there was a guard shack, and right where a small dirt road joined a larger road, there were a couple of Iraqi Arab guards, like night watchmen. They were telling us in Arabic, "We don't know what's in that buried tank, but you should be real careful." They were carrying gas masks and handed some to us. We asked them, "Why do you have these gas masks?" They replied, "We don't know. The Republican Guard used to control that buried tank and they never let us come near it. Two days ago, the Republican Guard got in their vehicles. As they were leaving, they threw these gas masks at us and shouted, "Here—it's your problem now." The watchmen didn't even know how to put the gas masks on.

After that, we went over to the 26th Marine Expeditionary Unit; I wanted to lash up with the Marines and establish a new method of operation. The commander was out, however, someplace else in the city. I ended up talking with the MEU intelligence officer, their S-2. I explained what we'd found at the Al Kindi Research Complex and Nineveh Woods. For a whole bunch of reasons, we needed to secure Nineveh Woods: to find out what was there, and, of course, to prevent the insurgents who were already setting the city on fire from getting ahold of it.

The Marine S-2 had no idea what we were talking about. The Marines didn't know where Nineveh Woods was located. They had no translators, nothing to connect them to Mosul. We dug out our maps and showed them the location. Then we talked, again, about securing that area. The Marines understood the need to secure Nineveh Woods and the Al Kindi Research Complex, but were dominated by their need to secure the airfield. They couldn't expand their presence on the ground. Honestly, when they were done holding the airfield and keeping themselves secure, two thousand Marines would not have been able to secure anything else in Mosul.

Even before they started to find out what was in those chemical tanks, they needed to have guys with Mission Oriented Protective Posture [MOPP] gear and chemical test equipment. And there was no such unit in Mosul, at that time. So, as we'd done with the Al Kindi Research Complex, we detached another group of Kurds, another fifty *peshmerga*. Now, fifty guys couldn't really control Nineveh Woods, and we knew that as soon as they began to attract significant insurgent attention, we'd have to pull them out.

Just think of the alternate reality—if the formal surrender of Mosul had happened—with us sitting in the 5th Corps HQ compound by April 12, 2003, completely in control, with the entire city in a relative state of stability. If you'd wanted to know what was in Nineveh Woods, you could've asked the Iraqi Army 5th Corps commander, and he could've said, "Fine, here is my adjutant, and he will give you the complete records on everything that is stored there."

Waltemeyer's decision to not accept the surrender of 150,000 Iraqi Army soldiers, the mayor of Mosul, and the governor of Nineveh—the entire structure opposite KDP territory in the North, all of the former government under Saddam in Northern Iraq—had nothing but tragic consequences, all born of Rumsfeld's decision under Bush's command to prevent the CIA from accepting the surrender of any Iraqi Army unit in the Iraq War.

Bush was president and commander in chief when the U.S. military, under his command, walked away from the surrender of 150,000 Iraqi Army soldiers. Bush did not blink an eye, because you can't blink when you're asleep at the wheel. Nothing would have prevented other Iraqi Army units and governmental structures from emulating the successful, and formal, surrender of Mosul, had Bush exercised anything close to pragmatic, engaged, and decisive command in mid-April 2003.

Furthermore, Bush's plan of attack in Iraq did not allow for Coalition troops to control population centers—once again, divorced from reality—making a formal surrender from the Iraqi Army even more vital to victory and winning the peace.

Another factor that had an overwhelming impact in the North, as the war went down, was that Sam got crystal-clear guidance from Bush's White House that the United States did not want Kurdish *peshmerga* to go into Mosul and Kirkuk.

Sam and his team had known for well over a year that the Turkish General Staff wanted no Kurds to enter Mosul and Kirkuk. But the Turks wanted Saddam to remain in power for a long time, so they looked at any Kurdish *peshmerga* in Mosul and Kirkuk as a threat to Saddam's jackboot on Kurdish necks.

Sam continued:

Bush's plan, due to Turkish protests, did not allow the bulk of the troops up north, Kurdish *peshmerga*, to enter either Kirkuk or Mosul. In truth, in order to end Saddam's regime, Kurdish *peshmerga* had to enter both cities, and did. Without the Kurds, we never would've defeated Saddam. But the Lost Surrender of Mosul ensured that an insurgency would definitely arise in Iraq, and the Kurds were the first to tell us that.

One of the things we said over and over after Mosul and Kirkuk fell—and I repeated this personally to everyone at Langley when I went home—was,

"We did not destroy the Iraqi military in the north. They just dissolved and went home. There is no Mission Accomplished; there is Mission Goatfuck." I still have that picture of the T-55 that was on the road to Mosul. That tank had the muzzle cover on its main gun.

When I got back to headquarters in early May 2003, I kept using that picture as an example, saying, You have to understand what this tank means. This was driven as a taxi by Iraqis who were headed south, going home.

They rolled it out of their barracks and used it as a ride south. When this tank ran out of gas, they climbed off it and hitched a ride home.

There were no live rounds in any of the weapons, the machine guns or the main tank cannon.

And they never took the muzzle cover off the main tank cannon.

From the time they left their barracks, they were doing one thing: going home. They had no hate in them, and no desire to fight for Saddam. No desire to fight anyone, for that matter.

They weren't killed, wounded, or captured. That was true largely throughout Iraq, and certainly true of Northern Iraq and the 150,000-strong Northern Front of the Iraqi Army.

I kept telling people, especially at home: The U.S. government missed the chance to get the Northern Front's surrender in Mosul, but in a lot of respects, it doesn't matter. Because if you put the Iraqi Army 5th Corps commander on the radio tomorrow, and he says, "All units should report to their barracks tomorrow to receive their pay," the only problem that you are going to have is that at every regiment, you're going to be at 120 percent strength. And you're going to have to weed out the guys who are just looking for a handout, who don't belong to the regiment but are trying to get paid. You then hand every one of their guys rifles—don't give them back heavy weapons, artillery, air defense, and tanks—and assign them all to checkpoints and security. Attach an American Special Forces commando at every battalion level, and overnight you'll have 50,000 guys on the street in Mosul and Northern Iraq, taking care of law and order. Then you don't have looting, then you don't have chaos, then you don't have anarchy, then you don't have this firestorm that plunged us into the abyss in Iraq.

The U.S. government brought in a chief of station, CIA, Baghdad. It was like everyone we were talking to was giving themselves high-fives: "We kicked ass, we've won this thing." But the attitude among my team members was: "We've gone from securing the surrender of 5th Corps to blowing that opportunity, thanks to Waltemeyer, and the whole place is a madhouse."

By April 2003, we were in a guerrilla war in Iraq.

There was no control, no order, no civil authority.

We'd had to shift bases twice in Mosul because we were taking so much incoming.

Basically, what we saw was chaos, no plan, no control.

I remember every day in Salahuddin, seeing convoys of trucks carrying ammunition and weapons that Kurdish *peshmerga* had captured. Heavy artillery, tanks by the dozen.

Now the Kurds had an armor battalion, just in Salahuddin. Trucks full of captured RPGs and Kalashnikovs. Kurdish gun trucks rolling, manned by *peshmerga.* I remember thinking, *These guys know what is coming. The Kurds know it's not all sweetness and light.*

We were sending our messages back to headquarters, daily, warning that the United States was now in a guerrilla war in Iraq. And nobody, absolutely nobody stateside, was paying any attention.

Waltemeyer had ordered us to move all of our *peshmerga* out of Mosul. And we'd had this bizarre conversation with him: "How are we going to survive without our *peshmerga*? We've already been in a couple pitched battles."

Now, in mid-April 2003, headquarters ordered me to shut down Salahuddin and move everyone into Mosul. In Salahuddin, I had a base, secure communications, food and water, and security.

In Mosul, it was a street fight, night and day, 'round-the-clock guerrilla war.

I had guys sleeping in mountain bags, constant gunfire, no electricity, no water, no plumbing, and already, moving around Mosul was very difficult.

Headquarters began telling me, every day, "You must separate from the Kurds; you must have no *peshmerga* with you due to the symbolism of the U.S. being allied to the Kurds. The Kurdish areas don't exist anymore; we must not be lashed up with the KDP because we must only be lashed up with the Iraqi government."

I was thinking, "I don't even know how I am going to feed my people in Mosul. Now, headquarters is telling me to move the whole shooting match into Mosul. How am I going to support my team? With what electricity, food, and water?"

And, by the way, the Kurds have a slightly different opinion than Washington as to the continued existence of Kurdistan.

Headquarters was living in this fantasy world where we'd won the Iraq War and it was all champagne and high-fives. We were just wasting our time, talking to headquarters.

A senior clandestine officer came in from Jordan and said, "We don't need much CIA in Iraq now. We only need a half-dozen in Mosul, so you can bring everyone back. You guys keep talking about the Kurds, and you tell us that the U.S. is in a guerrilla war in Iraq, but that's bullshit. We're drinking champagne—we won the war." Again, totally divorced from reality.

The bulk of the team loaded up and flew out of Hareer on a U.S. Air Force C-17. We landed stateside in late April 2003. When I got back to headquarters, it was just more of the same, surreal attitude. They were all in this celebratory mode: "Wow! We won the war and everything is fabulous. More champagne—bring on the caviar."

I remember walking around the halls and talking to people, and having many conversations where it was painfully obvious that nobody wanted to hear anything that I had to say.

Nobody in Washington wanted to hear that Iraq was a smoldering mess.

And there were all these people just lining up to get on planes and fly into Baghdad who had no idea that they were flying into a guerrilla war. People who had had absolutely nothing to do with what had gone down during the previous year, nobody from any of my counterterrorist teams, none of the counterterrorists.

Nobody who had any knowledge of the operation went back in-country. The Agency's attitude was, "It's gravy at this point; now it's great."

I became chief of station in another country in the Near East. My Dahuk team leader never went back stateside. He just basically felt that he'd wasted enough time trying to talk sense into these assholes inside the Beltway for the last year, and he didn't want to see any of them. He stayed in the Near East, and took another assignment in counterterrorist operations.

Before I went on to my next assignment, the Qal'ah Chulan base chief and I talked about recognition for the people on our teams.

We said to Iraqi Operations Group, "Our proposal is that we should decide on a medal or decoration for everyone on the teams. And they should all be treated equally, except for those who really distinguished themselves."

Iraqi Operations Group said, "That makes sense. We'll decide on an appropriate medal, and make sure you tell us which ones should receive higher recognition." We selected four counterterrorist officers for the Intelligence Star: two for their actions against Ansar al-Islam in late March 2003, and two for their actions around Mosul in March and April 2003. The decorations were supposed to have been given out within ninety days.

Sixteen months later, the Iraqi Operations Group did give the Intelligence Stars out to all four guys, but they completely dropped the ball on everyone else. Iraqi Operations Group lost the list. It's as if those clandestine officers had never even set foot in Iraq. Then, Iraqi Operations Group gave decorations for gallantry and courage to people who had been stateside for the entire operation. I was furious about this, and for several months thereafter, told headquarters, "We have all these guys who were brave and gallant in the field, and you didn't recognize them, but you gave medals to people who never left their desks stateside." Headquarters told me to shut the fuck up.

At the end of the day, looking back at the entire operation, I was fortunate to keep my word to the Kurds, and it was an honor and a privilege to lead the counterterrorists on a clandestine operation that led directly to the fall of one of the most brutal dictatorships in the history of mankind.

EPILOGUE:

You Don't Win A Street Fight Throwing Jabs

by Mike Tucker

"There are worse things than war and they all come with defeat."

—ERNEST HEMINGWAY

Guerrilla war is nothing but a street fight, taken to another level. We are in a global guerrilla war against Al-Qaeda and all allies of Al-Qaeda, and the rules of guerrilla war are the same as in street fighting:

1. **You don't win a street fight throwing jabs.**
2. **The only dirty fight is the one you lose.**
3. **Put the other guy down so that he stays down.**
4. **Know your enemy:** know the terrain, turf, and tongue.
5. **Better to make a good run than a bad stand.** When you live to fight another day, you live to win on that day.
6. **Never let your ego command your judgment.** It's no accident that Odysseus survives in *The Iliad* and Achilles does not. For Odysseus, unlike Achilles, pride was not a virtue. Like General Ulysses S. Grant, Odysseus valued humility, candor, stamina, savvy, guile, listening skills, and boldness. Pride kills the soul that carries it.

7. **Survival is victory.**

When you're drinking coffee
with the one you love,
you're feeling no pain—
when God created women,
He must have been drinking champagne.

Odysseus understood the value of survival and drinking coffee with the one he loved, Penelope. As Lieutenant Colonel Daniel Sullivan, United States Marine Corps, infantry, said in Fallujah on January 13, 2006, "Odysseus was the first Marine; he knew how to out-think and out-fight the enemy. He valued guile and boldness and he brought out the brass knuckles when those idiots messed with his woman. Long live Odysseus."

Unlike Grant and Odysseus, Bush never fought our generation's war with a street fighter's cleverness, guile, savvy, resolve, and will. The United States must now contend with a resurgent Al-Qaeda that regained key terrain in Afghanistan during Bush's era, gained control of large areas of Pakistan, and is stronger than ever before.

In October 2008, the greatest division in our generation's war remains the divide between Americans who are going in harm's way and those who are not sacrificing to defeat and destroy Al-Qaeda. That divide is deeper than the Grand Canyon, and should it continue, it will not take Al-Qaeda to destroy America in order for Islamist terrorism to prevail: America will self-destruct.

As U.S. Marine Corps Captain Martin Keogh said on November 22, 2007: "We are going the way of Rome, with an extraordinary gap between those who are going in harm's way to save the American republic, and the vast majority who are not: that is a recipe for self-destruction in the United States, as it was clearly at the root of Rome's road to self-destruction, ruin, and defeat."

President Abraham Lincoln, like Keogh, understood the relationship between unity, sacrifice, and survival. As Lincoln said, *"A house divided cannot stand."* That is just as true of America in 2008 as it was in 1860. We are a house divided that will not stand if we do not come together as one people and one nation to slay the dragon of Al-Qaeda. The country that stands together, fights together, bleeds together, suffers together, and sacrifices together is the country that wins wars together.

American men and women are going in harm's way in Afghanistan and Iraq, night and day. They are the September 11th Generation and they represent less than one percent of Americans of fighting age.

As Marine scout/sniper team leader Derrick Boyer said in Fallujah in 2006, "This is our generation that is bleeding here." After the worst assault on the American homeland since 1775, men like Boyer did not hesitate to volunteer. The September 11th Generation deserves victory over Al-Qaeda, now.

As the Zen Buddhist proverb states, *"Now means now."* After Pearl Harbor, Franklin D. Roosevelt—unlike Bush after September 11th—called on all Americans to sacrifice in a war of survival. FDR understood the fierce urgency of now and an ancient truth of guerrilla war and street fighting, which is that once someone draws first blood on you, you must strike and kill them without hesitation. And because FDR, General George S. Patton, and General Douglas MacArthur were in accord on the fierce urgency of now, the United States and our allies prevailed in a war of survival won by the Greatest Generation. The covenant of the Greatest Generation—*Stand with me, bleed with me, and win with me: We will win this war together*—led America to victory from December 7, 1941, to September 2, 1945. To that end—achieving victory and ensuring the survival of the United States of America—a sea change is necessary for America to annihilate Al-Qaeda, the Taliban, and all of their allies.

SEA CHANGE: On Victory over Al-Qaeda

A) Constitutional Declaration of War, by law, signed by Congress and the President of the United States. If you ride with Al-Qaeda, you die with Al-Qaeda. Congressional Declaration of War against Al-Qaeda and all Islamist terrorist transnational armies allied with Al-Qaeda. Full mobilization of American people, industry, and government to this end: Death to Al-Qaeda and all allies of Al-Qaeda. WWII-era G.I. Bill.

B) End the Iraq War. Fight the Afghanistan War.

1) *Station U.S. Army 2nd Infantry Division (Thunderbird Division) and 10th Group Special Forces in Kurdistan.*

Lash up all U.S. military and intelligence assets with Kurdish intelligence, Kurdish military intelligence, Kurdish counterterrorist officers, and Kurdish police. Total U.S.-Kurdish counterterrorist lash-up.

Sign permanent security agreement with the Kurds. Near East counterterrorism command center would be Dahuk, Kurdistan.

Back Kurdish independence 10,000 percent, remove all Turkish military from Kurdistan, and with Kurdish Democratic Party political officers on point, end the PKK as a terrorist group: Use all U.S. assets and contacts who have deep ties and relationships to the Kurds—U.S. Army Special Forces and U.S. ambassador Peter W. Galbraith, to begin with—to bring Turkey and Kurdistan together to sign a peace treaty.

2) *End the Iraq War.* Support a three-state solution to Iraq and end U.S. efforts to perpetrate the failed British foreign policy, Churchill's self-professed greatest mistake, of forcing the Kurds to be ruled by Arabs and a central government in Baghdad. Move all U.S. State Department diplomats and assets to Dahuk, Erbil, and Kirkuk. Remove all U.S. combat forces from Central, Western, and Southern Iraq by June 2009.

3) *Iraq is a map, not a country.* End failed U.S. effort in Iraq in the twenty-first century, which is a mirror image of the failed British effort in the twentieth century, to force three vastly different cultures into one jury-rigged nation

in order to please Sunni Arab sheikhs in Saudi Arabia, Syria, and Jordan, and in order to please Turkey.

4) *Culture transcends politics and all things political, including money.* The Iraq War is breaking the back of the U.S. military in our fight against Al-Qaeda and Islamist terrorists.

We can spend the next four years in the Near East perpetrating the British failure over the last eighty-eight years in Iraq, or we can acknowledge the reality on the ground in the Near East: that three diverse cultures dominate three different landscapes in the heart of the Near East.

No amount of money, geopolitical constructs, realpolitik posturing, or neoconservative chicken hawk dogma will ever change the fact that ending Saddam Hussein's Baathist dictatorship opened the door to Kurdish independence and the end of Iraq. Nothing in the last eighty-eight years suggests that the interests of the Kurds and Shia, 80 percent of Iraq, will be served by the nation-state of Iraq.

Additionally, the Iraq War is bankrupting the American treasury and creating trillions of dollars' worth of debt. The fifteen billion dollars a week spent in Iraq, and the immense amount of time and energy wasted on the Iraq War by U.S. troops guarding reconstruction aid, will be far better spent on domestic U.S. counterterrorism and in Afghanistan.

5) *Fight the Afghanistan War.* Rules of Engagement: War. Sign permanent security agreements with Afghanistan and India. End all aid to Pakistan. End all aid to Saudi Arabia. End all aid to governments such as Pakistan, which support Islamist terrorism and allow Islamist *madrassas* to preach death to Americans and death to the United States of America.

Fight and win the war in Afghanistan following the template of two successful guerrilla wars in the Near East and Central Asia over the last fifty years: "Operation Storm," British SAS and British Intelligence (MI6), 1964–1976, and the Kurdish guerrilla war against Iraq, 1961–2003.

Train and equip the Afghan National Army as a guerrilla army. Increase aid and assets toward the Afghan National Army by 500 percent.

Recruit and deploy European, American, African, Arab and Asian nurses, doctors and veterinarians, lashed up with British SAS, together with the Afghan Army, throughout all of Afghanistan (as the SAS did in Oman, with great success).

Increase European, Asian, and American educational aid, medical aid, housing and developmental aid by 1,000 percent. Demine the valleys, roads, and mountains of Afghanistan. Dig wells and build irrigation canals throughout all of Afghanistan. Build universities in Kandahar, Mazar-e-Sharif, Kabul, and Tora Bora. Build an Afghan college system, modeled on the state college system in the Royal Kingdom of Thailand.

Fight and win the guerrilla war in Afghanistan with combat rules of engagement, and with very limited air support. The best ally the Taliban and Al-Qaeda have inside Afghanistan is the U.S. military's air strikes, which have turned many Afghans against the Karzai government and against the U.S.-led coalition in Afghanistan.

Arm every U.S. fire team with two grenade launchers, one light machine gun, and one automatic rifle. Arm every U.S. rifle squad with one 60mm mortar team. Arm every U.S. rifle platoon with five three-man sniper teams and two 81mm mortar teams. Arm every U.S. rifle platoon with five antitank/bazooka teams. Require that every U.S. sniper is also a demolitions specialist, meaning that sniper teams can also carry out sabotage actions against the Taliban and Al-Qaeda, and additionally, destroy all captured munitions of Taliban and Al-Qaeda.

All U.S. small arms ammunition will start with 7.62x 51mm (NATO round) caliber. Stopping power and lethality will be the benchmark for all U.S. small arms. Arm all U.S. Army and Marine infantry with an assault rifle that is 7.5 pounds with a thirty-round clip jacked in, which will fire 7.62, lethal and accurate, out to 600 meters.

The contracting system, as with all revised procurement for all U.S. weapons, will not be based on lowest bidder or highest amount of lobbyists knocking on Pentagon doors.

The contracting system will focus on three needs, in order of priority, as with all small arms: stopping power, accuracy, and lethality. Teach American infantry to shoot to kill, not shoot to wound.

Strike and kill Taliban and Al-Qaeda at every opportunity. Our mission in Afghanistan is to destroy the Taliban and Al-Qaeda, as our mission globally is to destroy Al-Qaeda and all Islamist terrorist allies of Al-Qaeda.

Deploy U.S. Army 10th Mountain Division, 173rd Airborne Brigade, 82nd Airborne Division, and 101st Airborne Division to Afghanistan's border provinces with Pakistan.

Stay on patrol night and day, stay on deep reconnaissance night and day, hold down every village night and day; disarm every village, hold every mountain pass, and kill every Taliban and Al-Qaeda terrorist in Afghanistan. If necessary, declare war on Pakistan and strike and kill Al-Qaeda and Taliban in their sanctuaries in Pakistan's Northwest Frontier and Baluchistan.

C) America would sign the Kyoto Agreement on Global Warming, appoint Nobel Peace Prize recipient Al Gore as global warming czar, focus on global initiatives to decrease carbon emissions, and sign the International Ban on Land Mines. Ending global warming in our time is essential in order for mankind and endangered species to survive—indeed, mankind is now an endangered species, threatened with extinction by global warming. The International Ban on Land Mines would have real teeth in it, with U.S. participation, and save millions of lives, worldwide.

D) National Service for all American men, eighteen to twenty-four years of age, as follows, with no exemptions for college, graduate school, law school, or other postgraduate education (the only exemptions would be physical, i.e., being declared "4F"). American men of draft age would serve four years in the U.S. military, Border Patrol, or International Demining Corps. Conscientious objectors would serve eight years in the VISTA program, domestically, or eight years in the Peace Corps, internationally.

1) *International Demining Corps.* With 200,000 Americans in an International Demining Corps, the United States would be on the tip of the spear, globally, to remove and destroy all land mines and other unexploded ordnance, starting in Cambodia, Laos, Vietnam, Afghanistan, Iraq, Kurdistan, Colombia, and other mined lands. The International Demining Corps would be one million strong, with men and women from all United Nations members eligible to serve. Americans of draft age would be eligible for the International Demining Corps, on four-year enlistments, as would American volunteers, ages eighteen to forty. Preference for volunteers would be given to U.S. military veterans with experience in demolitions. The UN would provide 80 percent of the funding for the International Demining Corps, along with 80 percent of the volunteers and administration.

2) *VISTA and Peace Corps.* Americans of draft age who are conscientious objectors would be eligible for VISTA and the Peace Corps, on eight-year enlistments. VISTA and the Peace Corps would be expanded three-fold, with VISTA's mission being to help train, educate, and develop Appalachia, rural America, and our inner cities. The Peace Corps would continue to train and educate people in underdeveloped countries, with a significant increase in countries and continents devastated by AIDS, such as Africa, India, Cambodia, and Thailand.

3) *Counterterrorism Tax.* All purchases in the United States and its territories would be taxed at 1 percent, with that 1 percent tax going directly to funding the U.S. military, FBI, and the new OSS counterterrorism operations in America and worldwide, International Counterterrorist Command, the International Demining Corps, VISTA, and the Peace Corps, and to invest in alternative energy sources, such as photovoltaic solar power, hybrid fuels, and windmills.

4) *Convene International Meeting on Nuclear Weapons, with the goal of eliminating nuclear weapons from the world.* All nations in possession of nuclear weapons would be invited. Full court press on bringing the late U.S. president Ronald Reagan's best initiative—zero nuclear weapons in the world—from dream to reality. Eliminating nuclear weapons and the need to safeguard

and secure nuclear stockpiles would save the United States billions of dollars.

5) *International Counterterrorism Command.* The Cold War demanded NATO; this war demands an International Counterterrorism Command. Each area of the world would fall under a joint U.S./local counterterrorist command.

6) *Full recognition of Cuba.* One hundred percent lash-up with the Cuban government: diplomatic, economic, military, and counterterrorism.

Ending the U.S. embargo and isolation of Cuba will create a sea change in American relations with the Caribbean, Mexico, Central America, and South America.

It would also aid American counterterrorist efforts immensely in Africa, where Al-Qaeda is growing in strength and financing, and where Cuba has extensive and broad-based human intelligence networks.

Cuba has invested heavily in health care in Africa, has deep economic ties to Africa, and is regarded by many African nations as a friend and fair trading partner.

Cuba will be one of the most strategic and effective American allies against Al-Qaeda if the United States first looks downrange on a long-term basis, and answers one question first, on any matter involving foreign relations with any country: Is this country a potential ally against Al-Qaeda, or is it funding, protecting, and aiding Al-Qaeda?

Cuba, unlike Pakistan and Saudi Arabia, does not fund, protect, or aid Al-Qaeda. Taking down Al-Qaeda in Africa is critical to American survival, and, furthermore, Cuba would aid America in ending Al-Qaeda's threat to Africa, Europe, America, and Latin America.

7) *Permanent security agreements* with Afghanistan, India, Kurdistan, Israel, Cuba, Singapore, Malaysia, Indonesia, the Philippines, the Royal Kingdom of Thailand, and our NATO allies, with full basing rights and total coordination and communication in the global counter-terrorist war.

8) *End U.S. foreign aid and all U.S. military aid to Saudi Arabia and Pakistan.*

E) Terminate the CIA and resurrect the OSS—integrate all U.S. intelligence assets into a re-engineered Office of Strategic Services. Appoint Richard Marcinko, former SEAL Team Six commander, guerrilla war genius, and a brilliant counter-terrorist, as Commander of the new OSS. Pay him one million dollars a year; pay his deputy commanders five hundred thousand dollars a year. Increase pay of the U.S. president and commander-in-chief to two million dollars a year. Unleash the OSS as the point element against Al-Qaeda and all Islamist terrorist transnational armies. Integrate Defense Intelligence Agency counterterrorist officers, immediately, into the OSS. The CIA has too much bureaucratic dead-weight to contribute effectively to taking down Al-Qaeda.

F) Full Court Diplomatic Press on Full Recognition of Israel by all UN Nations, and Full Court Diplomatic Press on a Palestinian State. Appoint the very best U.S. diplomats, such as Ambassador John Limbert (retired), as Near East envoys to build a road to peace and end the threat of destruction to the State of Israel. We must fully commit to forging what Sun Tzu refers to as the most important objective of any war: a peace that endures, a lasting peace.

G) End a new Cold War with China before it begins. The greatest danger to American survival comes from Saudi Arabia, Pakistan, Al-Qaeda, the Taliban, and all Islamist terrorists. China is not our enemy. Al-Qaeda and all Islamist terrorists are our enemy. Unlike China, Al-Qaeda has actually declared war on us and killed American citizens, in the thousands.

Mainland China, Taiwan, and the entire world will suffer tremendously if Al-Qaeda and allies of Al-Qaeda in the Far East sever shipping lanes and cause havoc, mayhem, and terror throughout Asia. The U.S. and China can act as partners for greater global peace by signing a nuclear non-proliferation treaty.

Allied with Russia, India, and China, the U.S. will defeat Al-Qaeda on mainland Asia. We share a mutual interest with China: the defeat of Islamist terrorism in all strategic trading chokepoints in Asia, such as the Straits of Malacca. China has no interest in Al-Qaeda prevailing in Afghanistan, nor anywhere else in Asia.

If we don't fight and win our generation's war, a global guerrilla war against Islamist terrorism, then the next-generation fighter jets, bombers, aircraft carriers, and submarines presently on the drawing boards of the military-industrial complex in Northern Virginia will be as strategically effective as ice in hell. Once we fight and win the war we are in, with total commitment from the American people, we will prevail.

Semper Fi.

GLOSSARY

Afghanistan, the war in Afghanistan: A landlocked country in Central Asia, bordered to the east by Pakistan, Afghanistan's historic trading routes link Russia to the Persian Gulf, India to Europe, and China to Europe and the Near East. Invaded and conquered since the time of Alexander the Great, Afghanistan was fought over and held by the British in the nineteenth century, and returned to Afghan rule in 1920.

King Zahir Shah ruled one of the few peaceful and stable eras in Afghan history, from 1928 to 1973, before he was deposed in a coup by his cousin, Mohammed Daoud. A little over six years later, on Christmas Day, 1979, Soviet tanks, fighter jets, bombers, and infantry invaded Afghanistan, the start of over thirty years of unending warfare. Radical Islamic jihadists from all over the world, principally from Saudi Arabia and North Africa, fought to end the Soviet-backed rule of the Afghan communist leader, Najibullah, and were funded by Saudi Arabian intelligence, Pakistani intelligence, and the U.S. Central Intelligence Agency, from the early 1980s to the early 1990s. Osama bin Laden, son of one of the wealthiest men in Saudi Arabia and a close friend of the Saudi royal family, recruited the Afghan jihadists for his Radical Islamic terrorist transnational army, Al-Qaeda, starting in the late 1980s. (See Steve Coll's *Ghost Wars* and Lawrence Wright's *The Looming Tower.*)

The United States made a few attempts to kill Osama bin Laden and Al-Qaeda's core leadership in the 1990s, during the second Clinton administration in the United States (January 1997 through January 2001), but all failed. President Clinton, like President Bush (until September 11th), never ordered America's premier counterterrorists, U.S. Army Delta Force and U.S. Navy SEAL Team Six, to strike and kill Osama bin Laden, despite the fact that Delta Force and SEAL Team Six were specifically created and trained to kill terrorists.

Pakistani intelligence (ISI) has never wavered in its commitment to Al-Qaeda and the Taliban, the party that seized Kabul on September 26, 1996, and during its radical Islamic rule in Afghanistan from fall of 1996 to December 2001, routinely beheaded Afghan women for the crime of walking to a market alone.

After the devastating Al-Qaeda assault on the American homeland on September 11, 2001, the United States, Great Britain, Australia, and Canada led a Coalition to defeat the Taliban and Al-Qaeda in Afghanistan. Coalition forces, spearheaded by CIA paramilitary commandos, U.S. and British Special Operations, and Australian Special Air Service, seized Kabul on December 11, 2001.

Osama bin Laden managed to escape the manhunt designed to capture him, as did the Taliban's leader, Mullah Omar, and Al-Qaeda's Egyptian-born operations commander, Ayman al-Zawahiri. Since the beginning of the Iraq War in March 2003, under President Bush's command, Coalition forces have lost one-third of Afghanistan back to the Taliban and Al-Qaeda. In September 2008, at the time of this writing, the Northwest Frontier of Pakistan, and Baluchistan, a

Pakistan province bordering southern Afghanistan, continue to be recruiting centers and armories for Al-Qaeda and the Taliban. Al-Qaeda and the Taliban own Pakistan's border with Afghanistan, and operate freely from their stronghold in Northwestern Pakistan.

Al-Qaeda: Radical Islamic terrorist group formed by Osama bin Laden in 1988, Al-Qaeda has now entered its third decade of terrorist operations worldwide as of September 2008. Main Al-Qaeda recruiting and operations centers are found in England, Egypt, Pakistan, Saudi Arabia, Syria, North Africa, Indonesia, the Philippines, Western Europe, East Africa, and all of the Near East, with the exception of Kurdistan and Israel. The religious and financial base of Al-Qaeda is Saudi Arabia, with Pakistan running a very close second.

Al-Qaeda murders people on any continent, in any port, and at high sea, using suicide bombers who employ small boats, trucks, jet planes, cars, motorcycles, jeeps, donkey carts, and their own bodies (wearing vests packed with plastic explosive and/or TNT). The predecessor of Al-Qaeda is the ancient radical Islamic sect known as The Assassins, which likewise cited Islamic jihad as justification for its suicide attacks, and like Al-Qaeda, used terrorism as a political tool, seeking political gains through suicide attacks in the eleventh and twelfth centuries in the Near East.

Founded by the Saudi Arabian fugitive Osama bin Laden in 1988, son of one of the wealthiest businessmen in the Near East, Al-Qaeda declared war on the United States in 1996. Like the Radical Islamic terrorist groups Hamas and

Hezbollah, each active since the 1970s, Al-Qaeda claims religious justification in the name of Islamic jihad for its suicide bombing attacks. *TIME* magazine reported in January 2006 that Al-Qaeda terrorists and other radical Islamic terrorists allied worldwide with Al-Qaeda now number between 50,000 and 54,000. *TIME*'s assessment has not been contested by the United States government or by allies of the United States.

Sworn to destroy the United States and to kill American citizens, anywhere on earth, Al-Qaeda has also sponsored or inspired many other radical Islamic terrorist attacks in the West since the devastating and barbaric September 11th attacks in America: the March 11, 2004, railway attack in Madrid, Spain, which killed 190 people; the Al-Qaeda terrorist Richard Reid's attempt to blow up a 747 jet passenger plane; the radical Islamic terrorist bombing in Bali, targeting and killing Western tourists (primarily Australian) in October 2002; and the horrific London subway and bus bombings on July 7, 2005, which killed 52 people and maimed and wounded hundreds more.

Al-Qaeda, at time of this writing in September 2008, remains fully committed to murdering people, including Muslims, in suicide attacks in order to achieve its political goals: the destruction of the United States, Israel, Great Britain, Australia, and all allies of the United States; the reestablishment of the Taliban as the radical Islamic ruling power in Afghanistan; and full power in Saudi Arabia, Egypt, and throughout North Africa and the Near East, with Al-Qaeda ruling Saudi Arabia directly.

CENTCOM: United States Central Command. Headquarters: Tampa, Florida. Main foreign base: Qatar. U.S. military nerve center for U.S. combat operations in the Near East, Horn of Africa, Arabian Peninsula, and Central Asia.

Central Intelligence Agency (CIA): Created to prevent another Pearl Harbor, the CIA was formed out of the remnants of the Office of Strategic Services (OSS), which had carried out clandestine operations, sabotage, and raids, globally, during WWII. President Truman disbanded the OSS in the fall of 1945, and signed the CIA into law in 1947. The CIA is bound by law to inform the American president and commander in chief of all threats to the American homeland and to American citizens.

Command-detonated: You see what you destroy by running a wire to the explosive and setting off the charge by hand.

CT (Counterterrorism): The art and craft of taking down terrorists and terrorist cells, preventing terrorist attacks, and destroying terrorist groups.

Delta Force: U.S. Army Special Forces Operational Detachment Delta, Combat Applications Group (SFOD-D, CAG). Modeled on the British Army Special Air Service Brigade (SAS). Primary mission is counterterrorism. Often carries out missions with U.S. Army Rangers in support. Founded in 1977 by Colonel Charles Beckwith, U.S. Army Special Forces. With U.S. Navy SEALS, tasked with military counterterrorism (see the U.S. Army Special Forces Delta veteran and author Eric Haney's terrific book, *Inside Delta Force*).

Eyes on, eyeball, scope: All terms that signify looking at something directly, and are all related to human intelligence—intelligence gained from human sources.

Field Intelligence, Intel: Intelligence gained in the field, from both human and technical sources, primarily human, and interpreted in the field. U.S. Army snipers, for instance, have a core mission to gather field intelligence, at all times, in combat.

Fighting knife: In this book, this term refers to any knife designed and forged for combat.

FLASH, or FLASH FLASH FLASH: U.S. military radio code, also used by CIA Directorate of Operations, meaning, *I am under fire.* When FLASH is the first word in a written message, it also indicates *Immediate action, now.*

Headquarters: Refers in this book to Langley, Virginia, headquarters of the Central Intelligence Agency.

IED (Improvised Explosive Device): Often dug into sides of roads, or beneath asphalt or dirt in the middle of a road, but also, simply placed in mud and under trash near sidewalks in Iraq and thrown out of taxis. Also known as a roadside bomb. Often placed in carcasses of dead animals. Detonated by remote control, cell phones, and other electronic means, and also, command-detonated.

In the black, put it in the black: Shoot a bull's-eye or center mass.

Iraq, the Iraq War: Drawn by British mapmakers in London in 1919 from the former Mesopotamia, which was part of the Turkish Ottoman Empire, Iraq, throughout the twentieth century and the first decade of the twenty-first century, became a battleground between three very distinct peoples—the Sunni Arabs, the Shiite Arabs, and the Kurds—forced by the British to be ruled by a central government in Baghdad. Sunni Arabs, heavily supported by British colonial rulers in order to please Sunni Arabs in neighboring Syria, Turkey, and oil-rich Saudi Arabia, held the reins of power in Iraq from 1920 to 2003.

Roughly 20 percent of Iraq is Sunni Arab, 20 percent Kurdish, and the remaining 60 percent, Shiite Arab. The Baathist dictatorship of Saddam Hussein, dominated by Sunni Arabs, murdered over 300,000 Kurds and Shiite Arabs between 1978 and 2003, including summary executions of political prisoners at Abu Ghraib prison (see the author's *Hell is Over: Voices of the Kurds after Saddam*).

One of the most accurate observations of Iraq was made by Gunnery Sergeant Harrington of Fox Company, Second Battalion Sixth Marine Regiment, in Fallujah, Western Iraq, on March 22, 2006: "Under Saddam, 20 percent of this country, the Sunnis, fucked over 80 percent of this country: the

Shiite and the Kurds. And that 80 percent, the Shiite and the Kurds, are never, never going to let the people who raped their mothers and murdered their fathers back into power, running the show from Baghdad or any other city."

The Iraq War has been referred to by U.S. troops in-country with many names; however, the appellation given it by Marine Scout/snipers and Marine infantry in Fallujah in the winter of 2005–06 strikes the bull's-eye: "Bush's Goat Fornication." President Bush ordered the invasion of Iraq on March 19, 2003, to end the Baathist dictatorship of Saddam Hussein; Bush's main argument to the United Nations and the world was that Saddam Hussein, in violation of UN resolutions, continued to possess chemical, biological, and nuclear weapons of mass destruction. Baghdad was seized but not secured on April 9, 2003, by elements of the U.S. Army 3rd Infantry Division and 1st Marine Division. The capture, and subsequent hanging, of Saddam Hussein for his war crimes did not end the Iraq War. At the time of this writing in September 2008, no weapons of mass destruction have been found in Iraq.

Iraqi Army, IA, IAs: All terms for Iraqi Army soldiers.

Iraqi Police, IP, IPs: The Iraqi Police.

Islamic: Referring to the Muslim faith, Islam, which follows the Koran as its holy book; believes there is no God but Allah and he is the one God; and honors the Prophet Muhammad, Peace Be Upon Him. Along with Judaism and

Christianity, Islam is one of the three main religions born in the Near East. Prior to the Taliban, Islam had no quarrel with Buddhism in Afghanistan, going back to the time of the Prophet Muhammad; however, under the Taliban's rule in Afghanistan (1996–2001), the legendary and renowned Buddhist statues in Bamiyan were destroyed with Taliban artillery fire, and Buddhist relics and artifacts were similarly reduced to ashes.

Islamist: Often referred to with the phrase **Radical Islam.** *Islamist* denotes anyone or any organization, such as Osama bin Laden, the Muslim Brotherhood, Al-Qaeda, Hezbollah, and Jemaah Islamiyah, who is at war with the United States and its allies, and seeks the destruction of Israel, the United States, and its allies. Islamists are also waging war to return the Taliban to power in Afghanistan, with Al-Qaeda's operational, recruiting, and training headquarters and bases fully restored in alliance with the Taliban, and for Islamist governments to gain power in Lebanon, Turkey, Egypt, all of North Africa and East Africa, Pakistan, India, the Arabian Peninsula, former Mesopotamia, Great Britain, and all Southeast Asia.

Islamists are often called jihadists in Europe, Africa, and Asia, for their devotion to holy war (*jihad*) as a means of pleasing Allah. Islamists have also been referred to as **Muslim fundamentalists** and **Islamic militants.**

Islamist terrorist: Any Islamist who kills non-Muslims and Muslims alike, in order to please Allah and gain eternal life in Paradise. Islamist terrorists interpret phrases from the Koran and sermons by Islamist clerics who support them in order to justify terrorist attacks such as September 11th, the Madrid train massacre in March 2004, and the London subway and bus massacres on July 7, 2005.

Islamist terrorist groups began nine hundred years ago, in the eleventh century AD, with The Assassins, in Syria, Mesopotamia, and Persia (present-day Syria, Western Iraq, Baghdad, Southern Iraq, and Iran). Contemporary Islamist terrorist transnational armies, which plan, finance, and execute mass murders worldwide, include Al-Qaeda, Jemaah Islamiyah, and Abu Sayyaf, in the Far East. Other phrases used for Islamist terrorists by many Near Eastern scholars have been **jihadists, radical Islamic terrorists, Islamic militants, and Islamist extremists.**

Muslim counterterrorists in Kurdistan, who pray to Allah, venerate the Prophet Muhammad, and attend Kurdish mosques, are the most successful counterterrorists against Islamist terrorists.

Kurdish Muslim counterterrorists, utilizing a human intelligence network that extends to mosques, banks, churches, synagogues, markets, and schools, have killed more Islamist terrorists than any other counterterrorist group in the Near East; stopped suicide bomb attacks from happening, in droves; taken down Hamburg cells of Al-Qaeda; and are responsible for the virtual absence of Al-Qaeda and other Islamist terrorists in Kurdistan since August 2004.

Know for a fact: U.S. military slang for, *This is true, knowledge gained firsthand.*

Know this: U.S. military slang, which means, *What I am about to tell you is true.*

Kurdistan: Autonomous region of Northern Iraq, defined geographically by the Gara and Zagros mountain ranges, settled by the Kurds for over 6,000 years. The Kurds of Iraq, led by Mala Mustafa Barzani, declared revolution on September 11, 1961, to forge a nation. On October 15, 2005, 98 percent of the Kurds voted in favor of Kurdish independence from Iraq (see Peter Galbraith's *The End of Iraq*).

Langley: Also refers in this book to CIA Headquarters at Langley, Virginia.

Light Infantry, light infantrymen: In this book, both terms refer to 10th Mountain Division soldiers and commanders. Skilled on all small arms and heavier weapons, such as mortars, rocket launchers, and heavy-caliber machine guns, light infantrymen move hard and fast on foot on any terrain, and can patrol on deep reconnaissance and carry out other Special Operations missions when trained and tasked.

M4: U.S. Army assault rifle. Fires 5.56mm (NATO). The M4 has a telescopic buttstock, is lightweight and reliable, and pops up quick on your shoulder. Excellent for urban combat, and for jungle, desert, and mountain combat. Superior to the U.S. Marine infantry M16A-4 in every way but stopping power (both rifles fire a varmint round, 5.56). U.S. Army rifle teams at Fort Benning have fired bull's-eyes with the M4 at 800 meters.

M4/M203: The M4/M203 assault rifle/grenade launcher, which fires both 5.56mm ammunition and 40mm grenades. Combat effective range for the M203 grenade launcher is 300 meters. First fielded in the Vietnam War, the M203 grenade launcher is the most versatile small-arms weapon fielded by the U.S. military. Issued to U.S. Army infantry, all U.S. Special Operations, and to U.S. Marine Force Reconnaissance and Reconnaissance units. Marine infantry carries the M16A-4/M203.

M240B 7.62x51mm (NATO) medium machine gun: The work-horse of U.S. Army infantry, a fairly heavy machine gun for light infantry but with an excellent reputation for not breaking down in combat. Mounted on gun trucks and also carried on foot patrols by U.S. Army infantrymen. Referred to as a *machine gun.*

Rangers: *See* U.S. Army Rangers.

Rangers Lead The Way!: Motto and core philosophy of U.S. Army Rangers, who never hesitate to carry the fight to the enemy. In their philosophy and actions, the Rangers resemble the Spartans of ancient Greece.

Remote-detonated: You don't have to see what you are destroying. A cell phone operated five miles away from an IED can be used to remote-detonate the IED.

Roadside bomb: *See* IED.

SAW M249 5.56mm (NATO) light machine gun: Squad Automatic Weapon (SAW) for U.S. Army infantry and U.S. Marine infantry. Referred to as a light machine gun.

September 11th: On September 11, 2001—on orders from the terrorist leader of Al-Qaeda, Osama bin Laden—nineteen Al-Qaeda terrorists, fifteen of whom were from Saudi Arabia, hijacked United Airlines and American Airlines passenger jets taking off from Boston, Massachusetts; Newark, New Jersey; and Dulles, Virginia. Bound for the West Coast, each passenger jet was top-loaded with fuel. Carrying box cutters, the Al-Qaeda terrorists penetrated airport security, boarded the first-class section in each jet, and once in flight, sliced the throats of pilots and passengers, commandeered the jets, and carried out their suicide attacks on the World Trade Center in New York City, the cultural and financial capital of the United States, and the Pentagon, U.S. military headquarters, directly south across the Potomac River from Washington, D.C.

Passengers on United 93, hearing on their cell phones that the other hijacked planes had crashed into the World Trade Center and Pentagon, fought back against the Al-Qaeda terrorists on board; in the chaos and struggle, United 93 crashed in a field in Western Pennsylvania. Consensus among historians of September 11th is that United 93 was headed to Washington, to destroy either the White House or the U.S. Capitol Building. As of May 2008, Osama bin Laden remains at large, reportedly in the remote, rugged mountains bordering Afghanistan and Pakistan.

Sidearm: In this book, *sidearm* refers to the U.S. Army issue 9mm Beretta semiautomatic pistol, which fires a 15-round magazine.

Special Forces: *See* U.S. Army Special Forces.

10th Mountain Division: Formed during WWII to raid, assault, seize, and hold mountain redoubts in Europe held by Nazi German and Italian forces, 10th Mountain Division has become, in our time, the most battle-experienced light infantry in the U.S. military. From the Battle of Mogadishu, when 10th Mountain light infantrymen rescued U.S. Army Rangers and Delta Force commandos on October 3, 1993, in the heaviest combat U.S. forces had seen since the Vietnam War, to Afghanistan and Iraq since September 11th, 10th Mountain Division has deployed more often than any other U.S. Army division. Their headquarters is Fort Drum, in upstate New York, about thirty miles south of the Canadian border.

U.S. Army: Foremost land fighting force of the United States, the U.S. Army was formed in the American Revolutionary War (1775–1781) under General George Washington, who crossed the Hudson in the fall of 1781 with the main body of the Revolutionary Army, led an epic forced march south, and won the war at Yorktown, Virginia.

The U.S. Army was pivotal in defeating the Imperial German Army in WWI and the Nazi German Army, the Japanese Imperial Army, and the Imperial Italian Army in WWII. Since September 11, 2001, the U.S. Army has been heavily engaged in Afghanistan, Iraq, the Horn of Africa, and with its Special Operations Forces, throughout the world. The majority of the Special Operations Forces in United States Special Operations Command (U.S. SOCOM) are U.S. Army forces: U.S. Army Special Forces, Delta Force, and U.S. Army Rangers. The U.S. Army 18th Airborne Corps, comprised of three legendary divisions—the 10th Mountain Division (light infantry), 101st Airborne/Air Assault Division, and 82nd Airborne Division—can raid from the sky with paratroopers and with very potent airmobile capabilities, by helicopter. General Ulysses S. Grant in the U.S. Civil War, General "Black Jack" Pershing in WWI, and General George S. Patton in WWII are some of the most respected U.S. Army commanders in U.S. history.

U.S. Army Rangers, Rangers: Legendary at raids and reconnaissance, the Rangers possess a remarkable battle record that extends back to the French and Indian Wars. Under Brigadier General William O. Darby in WWII, the Rangers led countless raids in North Africa, Italy, and Western Europe, and are famed for their actions at Pointe du Hoc, Normandy, France, on D-Day, June 6, 1944. Rangers are also paratroopers and exceptionally well skilled in Special Operations. A core mission for Rangers is to assault and secure hostile airfields. In our time, U.S. Army Rangers often support Delta Force on counterterrorist missions, and are highly skilled in all facets of Special Ops. The Rangers consist of three battalions: 1st BN 75th Rangers, based at Hunter Air Field, Savannah, Georgia; 2nd BN 75th Rangers, based at Fort Lewis, Washington;

and 3rd BN 75th Rangers, based at Fort Benning, Georgia. The 75th Ranger Regiment, one of the key elements in U.S. Special Operations Command (U.S. SOCOM) is presently engaged in Afghanistan, Iraq, and other terrain.

U.S. Army Special Forces, Special Forces: U.S. Army Special Forces were born of the U.S. and Canadian Special Service Brigade in WWII, which fought with great valor and distinction in Italy. U.S. Army Special Forces are masters of guerrilla warfare and have forgotten more than any other branch of the U.S. military can remember about counterinsurgency. Special Forces are presently engaged against Al-Qaeda, the Taliban, and other terrorists and insurgents in Afghanistan, the Near East, Africa, Europe, and the Far East.

U.S. Marine Corps: An elite American fighting force, founded at Tun's Tavern in Philadelphia on November 10, 1775. The Marine slogan, "First to fight," comes from their history of going on point in clandestine actions (U.S. Force Reconnaissance Marines), guerrilla war (U.S. Reconnaissance Marines and U.S. Marine infantry), and conventional war (all U.S. Marine forces). U.S. Marine Raiders in WWII laid the foundation for contemporary U.S. Marine Special Operations. In fall 2008, Marines are at war in Afghanistan and Iraq.

Vietnam War: 1961–1975. Also referred to in the Far East as the American Indochinese War, to distinguish it from the French Indochinese War (1946–1954). Won by the North Vietnamese Army and Viet Minh, the Vietnam War was both a guerrilla war and a conventional war, with the NVA and Viet Minh enjoying sanctuaries in Laos and Cambodia. Major Archimedes L. A. Patti, U.S. Army and OSS, wrote prophetic field intelligence analyses while on joint operations with Viet Minh guerrillas in 1945, which underlined the futility of trying to stop Ho Chi Minh from leading a united Vietnam to independence. Major Patti was ignored by the U.S. State Department in the first Truman administration (1945–1948). Over two million Vietnamese died in the Vietnam War, along with over 58,000 Americans.

Western Iraq: Known as Western Mesopotamia until the British changed the map in 1919, seizing Mesopotamia from the Turks' Ottoman Empire, and creating the map of Iraq. Western Iraq is strongly Sunni Arab, and the tribes in Western Iraq contributed significantly to the British-favored Sunni elite in Iraq. The Sunni Arabs of Western Iraq, and all Iraq, only numbered 20 percent of the country, but thanks in great part to British and American support, along with military and foreign aid from the Soviet bloc during the Cold War (1945–1989), the Sunnis controlled Iraq from 1920 until April 9, 2003, when Saddam Hussein's Baathist dictatorship fell to U.S.-led Coalition forces—without a formal surrender, however, from the Iraqi Army.

World War II (WWII): The Second World War, September 1, 1939–September 2, 1945. Began with Hitler's attack on Poland and his conquest of France and all Western Europe. British and Commonwealth forces were alone in leading global counterattack against both Nazi Germany and Imperial Japan until December 7, 1941, when the Japanese Navy's assault on Pearl Harbor, Hawaii, brought America into the war. Soviet communist forces, most notably in the Soviet victory at Stalingrad, were crucial to the defeat of Nazi Germany. General Dwight D. Eisenhower commanded Allied Forces in North Africa, the Mediterranean, Western Europe, and Northern Europe, and accepted unconditional surrender from Nazi Germany on May 1, 1945. General Douglas MacArthur, commander of all Allied forces in the Pacific, accepted unconditional surrender from the Imperial Japanese in Tokyo Bay on September 2, 1945, ending WWII.

BIBLIOGRAPHY

Aeschylus. *The Orestia.* Translator, Robert Fagles. New York: Viking, 1975.

Barr, James. *Setting the Desert on Fire: T. E. Lawrence and Britain's Secret War in Arabia, 1916–1918.* London: Bloomsbury, 2007.

Basho, Matsuo. *The Narrow Road to the Deep North.* Translator, Nobuyuki Yuasa. New York: Penguin, 1966.

Beowulf. Translator, Seamus Heaney. London: W. W. Norton & Company, Ltd., 2001.

Charriere, Henri. *Papillon.* Translator, Patrick O'Brian. London: Rupert Hart Davis, Ltd., 1970.

Coll, Steve. *Ghost Wars.* New York: Penguin, 2004.

Galbraith, Peter. *The End of Iraq.* New York: Simon & Schuster, 2006.

Gunaratna, Rohan. *Inside Al-Qaeda.* New York: Berkley, 2003.

Hemingway, Ernest. *Death in the Afternoon.* New York: Charles Scribner's Sons, 1932.

Hemingway, Ernest. *A Farewell to Arms.* New York: Charles Scribner's Sons, 1929.

Hemingway, Ernest. *For Whom the Bell Tolls.* New York: Charles Scribner's Sons, 1940.

Hemingway, Ernest. *The Old Man and the Sea.* New York: Charles Scribner's Sons, 1952.

Hemingway, Ernest. *The Snows of Kilimanjaro and Other Stories.* New York: Charles Scribner's Sons, 1964.

Hemingway, Ernest. *True at First Light.* London: William Heinemann, 1999.

Homer. *The Iliad.* Translator, Robert Fitzgerald. New York: Anchor Books, 1963.

Homer. *The Odyssey.* Translator, Robert Fitzgerald. New York: Anchor Books, 1963.

Jeapes, Tony, Major General. *SAS Secret War: Operation Storm in the Middle East.* London: Greenhill Books, 2005.

Lewis, Bernard. *The Assassins: A Radical Sect in Islam.* New York: Basic Books, 2003.

Manchester, William. *Goodbye, Darkness: A Memoir of the Pacific War.* New York: Little, Brown and Company, 1980.

McCullough, David. *1776.* New York: Simon & Schuster, 2005.

Newfield, Jack. *Robert Kennedy: A Memoir.* New York: Dutton, 1969.

Ninh, Bao. *The Sorrow of War.* New York: Riverhead Books, 1996.

O'Brien, Tim. *The Things They Carried.* New York: Houghton Mifflin, 1990.

Pirsig, Robert. *Zen and the Art of Motorcycle Maintenance.* London: The Bodley Head Ltd., 1974.

Saigyo. *Poems of a Mountain Home.* Translator, Burton Watson. New York: UP Columbia, 1991.

Shakespeare, William. *Four Tragedies: Hamlet, Othello, King Lear and Macbeth.* London: Penguin, 1994.

Shakespeare, William. *Henry V.* London: Penguin, 1994.

Sophocles. *Sophocles: The Complete Plays.* Translator, Paul Roche. New York: Signet Classics, 2001.

Suzuki, D. T. *Essays in Zen Buddhism.* New York: Grove Press, 1949.

Tucker, Mike. *Among Warriors in Iraq: True Grit, Special Ops and Raiding in Mosul and Fallujah.* Guilford, CT: The Lyons Press, 2005.

Tucker, Mike. *Hell Is Over: Voices of the Kurds after Saddam.* Guilford, CT: The Lyons Press, 2004.

Tucker, Mike. *In Kurdish Highlands and Other Poems.* Penang, Malaysia: Self-published, 2008.

Tucker, Mike. *The Long Patrol: With Karen Guerrillas in Burma.* Bangkok: Asia Books, 2003.

Tucker, Mike. *Remembering Hemingway and other poems.* Penang, Malaysia: Self-published, 2007.

Tucker, Mike. *RONIN: A Marine Scout/Sniper Platoon in Iraq.* Mechanicsburg, PA: Stackpole Books, 2008.

Tucker, Mike. *Straits of Malacca and other poems.* Penang, Malaysia: self-published, 2008.

Tzu, Sun. *The Art of War.* Edited and with foreword by James Clavell. New York: Delta, 1988.

Wiesel, Elie. *Night.* Translator, Marion Wiesel. New York: Hill and Wang, 2006.

Woodward, Bob. *Plan of Attack.* New York: Simon & Schuster, 2004.

Wright, Lawrence. *The Looming Tower.* New York: Alfred A. Knopf, 2006.

ACKNOWLEDGMENTS

Charles S. Faddis. CIA counterterrorist officer and case officer (retired).

Spanish Army counterterrorists. Siege of the Banco Central, Barcelona, Spain. May 23–24, 1981.

Lieutenant Colonel Daniel Sullivan, U.S. Marine infantry. Commanding officer, 1st Battalion 8th Marines, Camp Lejeune, North Carolina.

Lieutenant Colonel Joseph Felter, U.S. Army Special Forces and to all at Combating Terrorism Center, West Point.

Major Kirk Windmueller, U.S. Army Special Forces.

Captain Martin Keogh, U.S. Marine infantry.

RONIN Marine scout/snipers. Western Iraq, September 2005–April 2006.

Dr. Brannon Wheeler, Director of Center for Middle Eastern and Islamic Studies, U.S. Naval Academy.

Dr. Marina Favila, Shakespearean scholar and literature professor. James Madison University, Harrisonburg, Virginia.

Bill Finnegan, journalist and author. New York City.

The late Staff Sergeant Travis Twiggs, combat tracker and Marine.

The late Wing Commander Geoffrey Morley-Mower, British Royal Air Force, WWII. Literature professor, J.M.U., and author.

INDEX

ABOUT THE AUTHOR

Mike Tucker is a counterterrorism and guerrilla war specialist, poet, and Marine infantry veteran—and the author of eleven books. Among his works are Hell Is Over: Voices of the Kurds After Saddam (Lyons Press), a finalist for the 2005 Ben Franklin Award in History; Among Warriors in Iraq (Lyons Press); RONIN: A Marine Scout/Sniper Platoon in Iraq, named by the Salt Lake Tribune as one of the best nonfiction books since September 11; and six volumes of poetry. A former visiting lecturer at West Point, U.S. Naval Academy and visiting scholar on counterterrorism at James Madison University, he has led and witnessed counterterrorist raids in Spain, Burma, and Iraq; and patrolled on deep reconnaissance with Karen guerrillas behind Burmese Army lines. He lives in the Far East.